MALCOLM X

MALCOLM X

A GRAPHIC BIOGRAPHY

Written by Andrew Helfer · Art by Randy DuBurke

A NOVEL GRAPHIC from HILL AND WANG

A division of FARRAR, STRAUS AND GIROUX · NEW YORK

HILL AND WANG
A division of Farrar, Straus and Giroux
19 Union Square West, New York 10003

Serious Comics GNC, LLC
23 Bank Street, New York 10014

Distributed in Canada by Douglas & McIntyre Ltd.
Printed in the United States of America
First edition, 2006

Library of Congress Cataloging-in-Publication Data
Helfer, Andrew.
    Malcolm X : a graphic biography / written by Andrew Helfer ;
art by Randy DuBurke.—1st ed.
        p. cm.
    ISBN-13: 978-0-8090-9504-9 (hardcover : alk paper)
    ISBN-10: 0-8090-9504-1 (hardcover : alk paper)
    1. X, Malcolm, 1925–1965—Graphic novels. 2. Black Muslims—novels.
I. DuBurke, Randy. II. Title.

BP223.Z8L5745 2006
320.54'6092—dc22
[B]
                                                        2006013743

Produced by Jessica Marshall, Ph.D.
Lettering by Dan Nakrosis

www.fsgbooks.com
www.seriouscomics.com

1 3 5 7 9 10 8 6 4 2

MALCOLM X

TOWARD THE END OF HIS LIFE, MALCOLM X KEPT A LOADED RIFLE IN HIS HARLEM HOTEL ROOM.

WHEN A VISITING PHOTOGRAPHER ASKED HIM TO POSE HOLDING IT, HE AGREED.

HE PROBABLY KNEW THAT THE IMAGE OF AN ARMED BLACK MAN PREPARED TO DEFEND HIMSELF AGAINST ENEMIES "BY ANY MEANS NECESSARY" WOULD BE EMBRACED BY HIS FOLLOWERS, EVEN AS IT TERRIFIED WHITE AMERICA.

BUT THE RIFLE WASN'T SIMPLY A PROP— MALCOLM BELIEVED HE NEEDED IT FOR PROTECTION.

MALCOLM ALWAYS HAD ENEMIES, BUT THIS TIME WAS DIFFERENT. NOW HIS ENEMIES WERE BLACK MEN HE HAD ONCE CALLED HIS BROTHERS...

...AND THEY WANTED HIM DEAD.

MALCOLM X'S WORDS AND TEACHINGS HAD CHANGED THE LIVES OF MILLIONS OF AFRICAN AMERICANS.

THE NATION OF ISLAM, ONCE HIS STRONGEST SUPPORT, HAD REJECTED HIM.

BUT IN FEBRUARY 1965, HE KNEW THE END WAS FAST APPROACHING. EVERY DAY BROUGHT ANONYMOUS DEATH THREATS.

THE PREDOMINANTLY WHITE NYPD COULD NOT BE COUNTED ON TO PROTECT ITS FIERCEST CRITIC.

WITH ONLY A FEW REMAINING SUPPORTERS, MALCOLM WAS ESSENTIALLY ALONE AND UNGUARDED.

HE'D OFTEN SPECULATED THAT A VIOLENT DEATH WOULD BE HIS DESTINY. NOW HE WAS CERTAIN IT WAS ONLY A MATTER OF TIME.

BUT AS HE POSED FOR THE CAMERA THAT COLD FEBRUARY MORNING, THE WEIGHT OF THE RIFLE BALANCED IN HIS HANDS, HE MUST HAVE WONDERED:

HOW HAD IT COME TO THIS?

HE COULD ACCEPT DEATH FOR HIMSELF; HIS SOLE CONCERN WAS FOR HIS FAMILY'S SAFETY.

IN THE LARGEST SENSE, THE ANSWER HAD ITS ROOTS IN THE EARLIEST HISTORY OF AFRICANS IN AMERICA.

IT BEGAN WITH AFRICANS TAKEN FROM THEIR HOMES, PILED INTO SHIPS, AND TRANSPORTED TO THE SHORES OF AMERICA, TO BE SOLD INTO SLAVERY...

...AND CONTINUED UNTIL A HARD-FOUGHT CIVIL WAR BETWEEN THE STATES BROUGHT EMANCIPATION AND THE PROMISE OF EQUALITY.

BUT THE PROMISE WENT UNFULFILLED; THE HOPES FOR EQUAL TREATMENT UNDER THE LAW WERE DASHED.

IN THE DECADES FOLLOWING THE CIVIL WAR, LIFE FOR AFRICAN AMERICANS REMAINED CRUELLY OPPRESSIVE. THIS WAS TRUE ESPECIALLY IN THE SOUTH.

WHITE

COLORED

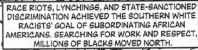

THERE, JIM CROW LAWS EFFECTIVELY SEGREGATED AFRICAN AMERICANS, KEEPING THEM SEPARATE AND UNEQUAL IN EVERY WAY.

WITH LOCAL AND POLICE APPROVAL, WHITE SUPREMACIST GROUPS LIKE THE KU KLUX KLAN TERRORIZED BLACKS, HELPING TO MURDER THOUSANDS.

RACE RIOTS, LYNCHINGS, AND STATE-SANCTIONED DISCRIMINATION ACHIEVED THE SOUTHERN WHITE RACISTS' GOAL OF SUBORDINATING AFRICAN AMERICANS. SEARCHING FOR WORK AND RESPECT, MILLIONS OF BLACKS MOVED NORTH.

LIFE, THEY HOPED, WOULD BE BETTER THERE.

CHAPTER ONE: *HARD TIMES*

MALCOLM'S FATHER, EARL LITTLE, WAS PART OF THIS MIGRATION. A CHILDHOOD SPENT IN GEORGIA, WHERE LYNCHINGS WERE FREQUENT, INSTILLED IN HIM A DESIRE FOR FREEDOM AND A CONVICTION THAT IT COULD NEVER BE WON IN WHITE AMERICA.

AS HE HEADED NORTH, HE WORKED AS AN ITINERANT PREACHER...

...FOR MARCUS GARVEY'S UNIVERSAL NEGRO IMPROVEMENT ASSOCIATION (UNIA).

GARVEY AND HIS FOLLOWERS PREACHED A POLITICAL GOSPEL OF BLACK SEPARATISM. THE UNIA BELIEVED THAT ONLY BY SHAKING OFF ALL WHITE INFLUENCES COULD AFRICAN AMERICANS TRULY BE FREE.

DECADES LATER, MALCOLM X WOULD FIND A SIMILAR SEPARATIST CAUSE IN THE NATION OF ISLAM (NOI).

MALCOLM'S MOTHER, LOUISE NORTON, WAS AS LIGHT-SKINNED AS EARL LITTLE WAS DARK. LOUISE'S BIOLOGICAL FATHER WAS A WHITE MAN WHO HAD RAPED HER MOTHER.

THE LITTLE FAMILY SETTLED IN OMAHA, NEBRASKA, WHERE EARL VISITED LOCAL BLACK CHURCHES TO PREACH GARVEY'S GOSPEL OF BLACK PRIDE AND SELF-SUFFICIENCY.

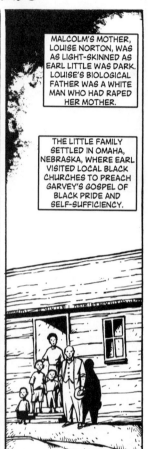

EARL'S "SUBVERSIVE" SPEECHES ATTRACTED THE ATTENTION OF THE OMAHA CHAPTER OF THE KU KLUX KLAN.

MALCOLM WROTE THAT JUST BEFORE HE WAS BORN, A GROUP OF ANGRY KLANSMEN CAME TO THE LITTLE HOME LATE ONE NIGHT, INTENDING TO BURN IT TO THE GROUND.

THEY WERE MET AT THE DOOR BY MALCOLM'S FIERCELY DEFIANT—AND QUITE PREGNANT—MOTHER, WHO SINGLE-HANDEDLY TURNED THEM AWAY.

THE KLAN'S THREATS STRENGTHENED EARL LITTLE'S RESOLVE TO SPREAD THE WORD OF GARVEY'S PLAN FOR AFRICAN AMERICAN SELF-SUFFICIENCY...

...EVEN THOUGH HE KNEW THIS GUARANTEED THAT THE KLANSMEN WOULD RETURN.

YEARS LATER, MALCOLM WOULD RETELL THE STORY AS AN EXAMPLE OF HIS PARENTS' COURAGE AND THE EVILS OF WHITE SOCIETY. HE BELIEVED IT FORESHADOWED THE DIRECTION HIS OWN LIFE WOULD TAKE.

HIS MOTHER, FOR HER PART, HAD NO MEMORY OF THE EVENTS.

ON MAY 19, 1925, MALCOLM LITTLE WAS BORN. EARL HAD LONG PLANNED TO NAME HIS SON AFTER HIMSELF.

BUT AFTER HIS FIRST LOOK AT THE INFANT, HE CHANGED HIS MIND.

HE LOOKS WHITE, LIKE HIS MAMA!

HIS NEW SON WAS NOT DARK-SKINNED ENOUGH TO TAKE HIS FATHER'S NAME. INSTEAD, HE WAS CALLED MALCOLM.

7

THE FAMILY MOVED SHORTLY AFTER MALCOLM'S BIRTH, FIRST TO MILWAUKEE AND THEN TO LANSING, MICHIGAN, WHERE EARL CONTINUED PREACHING FOR THE UNIA.

BLACK CONGREGATIONS APPLAUDED EARL'S MESSAGE BUT HAD SCANT MONEY TO GIVE HIM. STILL, BY 1929 THE LITTLES MANAGED TO BUY A SMALL FARMHOUSE.

THE FAMILY, HOWEVER, HAD PRECIOUS LITTLE MONEY TO MAKE ENDS MEET. EARL WAS FED BY GRATEFUL PARISHIONERS, BUT HIS WIFE AND CHILDREN OFTEN WENT HUNGRY.

TENSIONS GREW WITHIN THE FAMILY. EARL, NEVER A PATIENT MAN, BEGAN BEATING HIS WIFE AND CHILDREN AT THE SLIGHTEST PROVOCATION.

ONLY MALCOLM, FOR REASONS THAT HE BELIEVED HAD TO DO WITH HIS LIGHTER SKIN COLOR, ESCAPED HIS FATHER'S WRATH.

THIS ALREADY DESPERATE SITUATION SOON GOT WORSE. AGAIN, RACE WAS THE REASON.

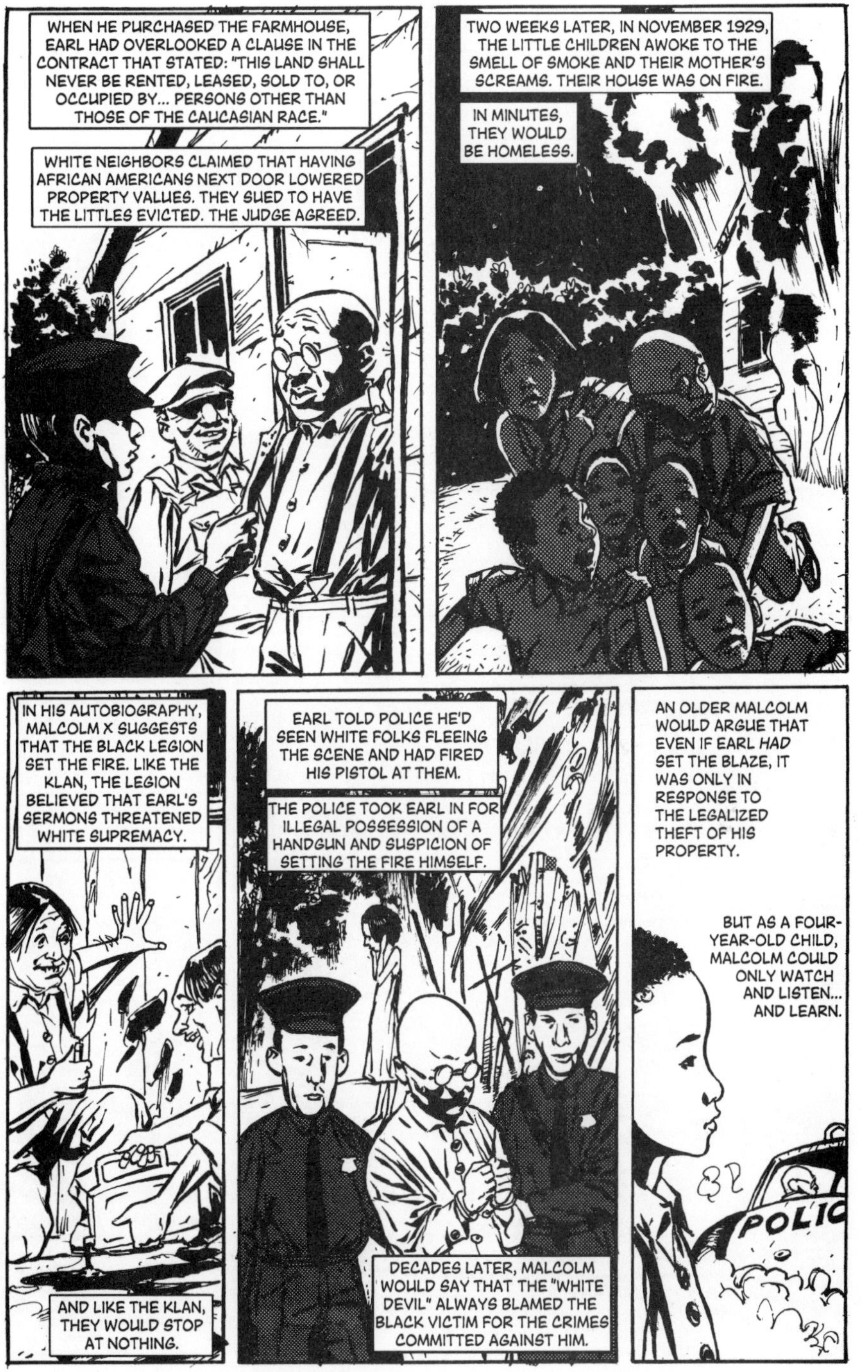
WHEN HE PURCHASED THE FARMHOUSE, EARL HAD OVERLOOKED A CLAUSE IN THE CONTRACT THAT STATED: "THIS LAND SHALL NEVER BE RENTED, LEASED, SOLD TO, OR OCCUPIED BY... PERSONS OTHER THAN THOSE OF THE CAUCASIAN RACE."
WHITE NEIGHBORS CLAIMED THAT HAVING AFRICAN AMERICANS NEXT DOOR LOWERED PROPERTY VALUES. THEY SUED TO HAVE THE LITTLES EVICTED. THE JUDGE AGREED.
TWO WEEKS LATER, IN NOVEMBER 1929, THE LITTLE CHILDREN AWOKE TO THE SMELL OF SMOKE AND THEIR MOTHER'S SCREAMS. THEIR HOUSE WAS ON FIRE.
IN MINUTES, THEY WOULD BE HOMELESS.
IN HIS AUTOBIOGRAPHY, MALCOLM X SUGGESTS THAT THE BLACK LEGION SET THE FIRE. LIKE THE KLAN, THE LEGION BELIEVED THAT EARL'S SERMONS THREATENED WHITE SUPREMACY.
AND LIKE THE KLAN, THEY WOULD STOP AT NOTHING.
EARL TOLD POLICE HE'D SEEN WHITE FOLKS FLEEING THE SCENE AND HAD FIRED HIS PISTOL AT THEM.
THE POLICE TOOK EARL IN FOR ILLEGAL POSSESSION OF A HANDGUN AND SUSPICION OF SETTING THE FIRE HIMSELF.
DECADES LATER, MALCOLM WOULD SAY THAT THE "WHITE DEVIL" ALWAYS BLAMED THE BLACK VICTIM FOR THE CRIMES COMMITTED AGAINST HIM.
AN OLDER MALCOLM WOULD ARGUE THAT EVEN IF EARL *HAD* SET THE BLAZE, IT WAS ONLY IN RESPONSE TO THE LEGALIZED THEFT OF HIS PROPERTY.
BUT AS A FOUR-YEAR-OLD CHILD, MALCOLM COULD ONLY WATCH AND LISTEN... AND LEARN.
POLIC

THE LITTLE FAMILY'S ATTEMPT TO RESETTLE ON THE OUTSKIRTS OF EAST LANSING, MICHIGAN, WAS MET BY MORE VIOLENCE FROM THEIR WHITE NEIGHBORS. THEY WERE FORCED TO MOVE AGAIN.

IN DECEMBER, THEY SETTLED ON SIX ACRES NEAR THE SOUTHERN EDGE OF THE CITY, AS THE GREAT DEPRESSION GAINED MOMENTUM.

AS THE DEPRESSION DEEPENED, EARL FOUND HIMSELF PENNILESS AND WITHOUT PROSPECTS. TENSIONS IN THE FAMILY GREW, OFTEN LEADING TO EXPLOSIVE VIOLENCE.

ON THE EVENING OF SEPTEMBER 28, 1931, EARL FOUGHT WITH LOUISE AND STORMED OFF INTO THE NIGHT.

A CALL FROM THE POLICE THE NEXT MORNING CONFIRMED LOUISE'S WORST FEARS: EARL LITTLE WAS DEAD, RUN OVER BY THE STEEL WHEELS OF A LANSING TROLLEY CAR.

IN HIS AUTOBIOGRAPHY, MALCOLM X BLAMED THE BLACK LEGION, THEY'D ATTACKED HIS FATHER, KNOCKED HIM OUT, AND SET HIS BODY ON THE TRACKS TO BE RUN OVER.

BUT EARL, WHO ACCORDING TO THE POLICE WAS STILL CONSCIOUS WHEN HE WAS FOUND, TOLD A DIFFERENT STORY:

I WAS RUNNING TO MAKE THE TROLLEY. I SLIPPED... THE REAR WHEELS MUST'A RUN ME DOWN...

WHETHER ACCIDENT OR MURDER, EARL LITTLE'S DEATH PLUNGED MALCOLM AND HIS FAMILY INTO THE DEPTHS OF DESPAIR AND POVERTY.

10

GRADUALLY, THE PRESSURE BECAME TOO MUCH TO FOR LOUISE TO BEAR. SHE WAS A PROUD WOMAN, AND WAS SHAMED BY NEEDING TO RELY ON CHARITY TO FEED HER CHILDREN.

NOT TO BE SOLD

SHE BEGAN A SLOW DESCENT INTO DEPRESSION, BECOMING LISTLESS AND ABSENTMINDED, WHILE NEGLECTING THE NEEDS OF HER CHILDREN.

WELFARE SERVICES, ALERTED TO LOUISE'S CONDITION, INTERVENED, DEALING THE FINAL BLOW TO THE LITTLE FAMILY.

LOUISE WAS JUDGED INSANE IN JANUARY 1939, AND WAS COMMITTED TO A MENTAL INSTITUTION.

THE CHILDREN WERE SPLIT UP:

THE YOUNGER CHILDREN, INCLUDING MALCOLM AND HIS BROTHER REGINALD, WERE SENT TO FOSTER HOMES...

...WHILE THE OLDER CHILDREN, WILFRED AND HILDA, WERE ALLOWED TO CONTINUE LIVING IN THE LITTLE HOME.

STARVATION WAS BEHIND MALCOLM— BUT MORE PROFOUND INDIGNITIES LAY AHEAD.

CHAPTER TWO: *RECKLESS YOUTH*

DESPITE THE BEST INTENTIONS OF HIS FOSTER FAMILY, MALCOLM DEEPLY RESENTED HIS NEW LIVING SITUATION. FRUSTRATED AND ANGRY, HE BECAME A DISCIPLINE PROBLEM AT SCHOOL.

A PRANK HE PLAYED ON HIS TEACHER CAUSED HIM TO BE EXPELLED. AT THE AGE OF 13, THE COURT ORDERED MALCOLM TRANSFERRED TO REFORM SCHOOL.

UNTIL A PLACE AT THE REFORM SCHOOL COULD BE SECURED, HOWEVER, MALCOLM WOULD BE SENT TO LIVE IN A NEARBY DETENTION HOME IN MASON, MICHIGAN.

THE HOME WAS RUN BY A WHITE FAMILY NAMED SWERLIN. PREVIOUS EXPERIENCES WITH WHITES HAD PREPARED MALCOLM TO EXPECT THE WORST, BUT HE WAS PLEASANTLY SURPRISED.

THE SWERLINS WERE KIND AND GENEROUS. THEY GAVE MALCOLM HIS OWN ROOM, ATE MEALS AT THE SAME TABLE WITH HIM, AND GAVE HIM THE FREEDOM TO TAKE DAY TRIPS TO LANSING TO VISIT FRIENDS AND FAMILY.

BECAUSE OF THIS, MALCOLM'S ATTITUDE TOWARD LIFE IN THE DETENTION HOME BECAME MORE POSITIVE.

THIS IMPRESSED THE SWERLINS, WHO ARRANGED FOR MALCOLM TO CONTINUE LIVING WITH THEM INSTEAD OF BEING MOVED TO REFORM SCHOOL.

MALCOLM WAS ENROLLED IN THE LOCAL PUBLIC SCHOOL, WHERE HE WAS ONE OF THE ONLY BLACK STUDENTS.

HE ALSO PROVED TO BE ONE OF THE SCHOOL'S BEST AND MOST POPULAR STUDENTS. IN THE SEVENTH GRADE, HE WAS ELECTED CLASS PRESIDENT.

BUT DESPITE HIS POPULARITY, THE SPECTER OF RACISM STILL HUNG OVER MALCOLM, BOTH IN SCHOOL AND IN HIS NEW HOME.

THE SWERLINS WERE RACIST IN SMALL, INSENSITIVE WAYS THAT STUNG THE YOUNG BOY. THEY USED THE WORD "NIGGER" IN THEIR JOKES WHEN GUESTS FROM TOWN WOULD VISIT.

THE JOKES WERE TOLD IN MALCOLM'S PRESENCE, WHICH MADE HIM FEEL MORE LIKE A FAMILY PET THAN A HUMAN BEING.

IN SCHOOL AS WELL, RACIST STORIES WERE COMMON — BOTH STUDENTS AND TEACHERS WERE FOND OF WHAT THEY BELIEVED WAS GOOD-NATURED RACIAL HUMOR.

THOUGH THE JOKES WERE TOLD AT HIS EXPENSE, MALCOLM REMAINED SILENT. HE LATER SAID HE WAS DESPERATELY TRYING TO FORGET THAT HE WAS BLACK, HOPING HE COULD SUCCESSFULLY INTEGRATE INTO THE WHITE WORLD AROUND HIM.

BUT IF MALCOLM BELIEVED HIS INTELLIGENCE AND POPULARITY HAD EARNED HIM AN EQUAL PLACE IN WHITE SOCIETY, HE WAS MISTAKEN.

THE LIMITS OF WHITE ACCEPTANCE WOULD BE MADE CLEAR TO HIM BY HIS ENGLISH TEACHER, WHO WANTED TO KNOW IF MALCOLM HAD THOUGHT ABOUT A CAREER AFTER GRADUATION.

WELL, YES, SIR, I'VE BEEN THINKING I'D LIKE TO BE A LAWYER.

MALCOLM, WE ALL LIKE YOU — BUT YOU'VE GOT TO BE REALISTIC ABOUT BEING A NIGGER.

YOU NEED TO THINK ABOUT SOMETHING YOU *CAN* BE.

YOU'RE GOOD WITH YOUR HANDS — MAKING THINGS. WHY DON'T YOU PLAN ON CARPENTRY?

PEOPLE LIKE YOU AS A PERSON — YOU'D GET ALL KINDS OF WORK!

THAT WAS THE MOMENT, MALCOLM LATER REMEMBERED, WHEN HE BEGAN TO CHANGE — INSIDE.

MALCOLM MASKED HIS ANGER AT WHITE SOCIETY BY EMOTIONALLY WITHDRAWING FROM IT. HIS SCHOOLMATES AND THE SWERLINS COULDN'T HELP BUT NOTICE THE CHANGE.

WHERE ONCE MALCOLM WAS FRIENDLY AND GREGARIOUS, NOW HE WAS COLD AND DISTANT.

MRS. SWERLIN BEGGED MALCOLM TO TELL HER THE REASON FOR THE CHANGE, BUT HE REFUSED TO DISCUSS IT.

BELIEVING THAT SHE WAS SOMEHOW RESPONSIBLE FOR HIS UNHAPPINESS, MRS. SWERLIN ARRANGED FOR MALCOLM TO MOVE IN WITH THE LYONS, A WEST INDIAN FAMILY WHO LIVED NEARBY.

THE LYONS RECEIVED A SIMILAR "SILENT TREATMENT" FROM MALCOLM. INSTEAD OF TALKING TO THEM, MALCOLM WROTE NUMEROUS LETTERS TO HIS HALF SISTER, ELLA, WHO OWNED A HOME IN BOSTON.

ELLA LITTLE COLLINS, MALCOLM WOULD LATER SAY, "WAS THE FIRST REALLY PROUD BLACK WOMAN I HAD EVER SEEN IN MY LIFE."

IT WAS A SENSE OF PRIDE IN BEING BLACK THAT MALCOLM NOW ASPIRED TO CARRY WITHIN HIMSELF. WANTING TO BE CLOSER TO ELLA'S GOOD INFLUENCE, HE ASKED TIME AND AGAIN TO LIVE WITH HER IN BOSTON.

MALCOLM KNEW HOW IMPORTANT FAMILY TIES WERE TO HIS HALF SISTER, SO HE WASN'T SURPRISED WHEN SHE AGREED. DURING A TRIP TO MICHIGAN, ELLA ARRANGED TO BECOME MALCOLM'S LEGAL GUARDIAN, AND THE TWO RETURNED TO BOSTON TOGETHER.

ELLA BROUGHT MALCOLM TO HER HOME IN THE SUGAR HILL SECTION OF ROXBURY, THE BLACK NEIGHBORHOOD OF BOSTON.

SUGAR HILL WAS THE ELITE PART OF THE NEIGHBORHOOD, HOME TO MANY OF ROXBURY'S WEALTHIEST BLACK PROFESSIONALS.

AT FIRST, MALCOLM WAS AWESTRUCK. HE'D NEVER VISITED A TRUE CITY, LET ALONE ONE IN WHICH BLACKS WERE CULTURED AND AFFLUENT.

BUT ONCE THE NOVELTY WORE OFF, MALCOLM BEGAN TO SEE THE RESIDENTS OF SUGAR HILL AS SELF-DELUDING IMITATORS OF WEALTHY WHITE SOCIETY.

MALCOLM REFUSED TO BELIEVE THAT THE ONLY WAY FOR A BLACK MAN TO BE TREATED AS AN EQUAL WAS TO "ACT WHITE." THERE HAD TO BE ANOTHER WAY—AND MALCOLM WOULD FIND IT.

REJECTING LIFE ON "THE HILL," MALCOLM VISITED THE ROXBURY GHETTO, WHERE HE DISCOVERED A LIFESTYLE MORE APPEALING TO HIS YOUNG SENSIBILITIES.

HE WANDERED THE STREETS, DRINKING IN THE SIGHTS AND SOUNDS OF THE CITY. HE SAW THINGS A COUNTRY BOY FROM MICHIGAN HAD NEVER DREAMED OF SEEING:

BILLIARDS

Dancing

KIDS GAMBLING ON STREET CORNERS...

ADULTS WITH STRAIGHT HAIR WEARING FANCY SUITS...

AND, MOST SHOCKING, BLACKS AND WHITES EATING, DRINKING, AND SOCIALIZING WITH ONE ANOTHER—IN THE SAME CLUBS.

THE EXCITEMENT WAS OVERWHELMING. MALCOLM WANTED TO BE A PART OF IT. BUT IN THIS STRANGE NEW WORLD, HE NEEDED A JOB—AND A GUIDE.

MALCOLM FOUND THAT IN A MAN HE LATER REFERRED TO ONLY AS "SHORTY." HIS REAL NAME WAS MALCOLM JARVIS.

YOU LOOKING FOR A JOB RACKING UP BALLS? DON'T KNOW ANY, RED.

HOW ABOUT SOMETHING ELSE? WHAT KIND OF WORK YOU DONE?

SOME DISHWASHING... UP IN MASON, MICHIGAN...

MY HOMEBOY! GIMME SOME SKIN! I'M FROM LANSING!

WITH THEIR COMMON ORIGINS TO BIND THEM, MALCOLM AND SHORTY BECAME FAST FRIENDS. PROMISING TO KEEP AN EYE OUT FOR JOBS...

...SHORTY SOON FOUND ONE FOR MALCOLM AS A SHOESHINE BOY AT THE FAMOUS ROSELAND STATE BALLROOM.

BUT A JOB WAS ONLY THE START OF MALCOLM'S STREETWISE EDUCATION. WITH TEACHERS LIKE SHORTY, MALCOLM WAS ON THE FAST TRACK.

THE MAIN THING YOU GOT TO REMEMBER IS THAT EVERYTHING IN LIFE IS A HUSTLE!

SIXTEEN-YEAR-OLD MALCOLM WANTED IN. BUT IF HE WAS GOING TO BE A HUSTLER, HE HAD TO LOOK THE PART.

EARNINGS FROM HIS SHOESHINE JOB PAID FOR HIS FIRST "CONK," THE PAINFUL HAIR-STRAIGHTENING PROCESS USED BY "REET, PETITE, AND GONE" BLACK HIPSTERS...

IIEEEEEE!!!! IT BURNS!! IT BURNS!!!

BUT EVEN AS HIS HAIR WAS STRAIGHTENED TO "LOOK WHITE," THE EXTRAVAGANT ZOOT SUIT HE PURCHASED HAD THE OPPOSITE EFFECT.

RATHER THAN EMULATING WHITE STYLE AND FASHION, URBAN BLACK HIPSTERS DISTANCED THEMSELVES FROM IT BY CREATING A UNIQUE ALTERNATIVE.

ON SOME LEVEL, THE NOTION OF CULTIVATING A CULTURAL IDENTITY APART FROM WHITES MUST HAVE APPEALED TO YOUNG MALCOLM—AT THE VERY LEAST, IT HELPED A GREEN COUNTRY BOY MIX WITH THE CITY'S OLDER COOL CATS.

BUT BEING A PART OF THE ROXBURY HIPSTER SCENE REQUIRED MORE THAN A FASHION STATEMENT.

IT REQUIRED, MALCOLM WOULD SOON DISCOVER, AN ENTIRE LIFESTYLE CHANGE—ONE IN WHICH "THE HUSTLE" WAS CENTRAL.

NEW FRIENDS LIKE SHORTY WERE ONLY TOO HAPPY TO EDUCATE MALCOLM. THEY INTRODUCED HIM TO THE PLAYERS ON THE STREET—FROM THE DOPE DEALERS TO THE PIMPS, GAMBLERS, AND SECOND-STORY MEN.

TO MALCOLM, IT SEEMED LIKE A WORLD OF OPPORTUNITY WAS OPENING—ALL HE HAD TO DECIDE WAS WHICH HUSTLE TO TRY FIRST.

SHOE SHINES

SO IN THE MEN'S WASHROOM OF THE ROSELAND BALLROOM, MALCOLM WENT TO WORK.

17

WITH HIS NEWFOUND CONNECTIONS, MALCOLM WAS THERE TO PROVIDE ANYTHING HIS CUSTOMERS DESIRED—DRUGS, ALCOHOL, NUMBERS, WOMEN— ALL FOR A PRICE AND A GENEROUS TIP.

THE PAY WAS GOOD ENOUGH FOR MALCOLM TO DECIDE NOT TO RETURN TO SCHOOL AND TO MAKE HUSTLING A FULL-TIME JOB.

AND WHEN HE WASN'T HUSTLING, MALCOLM WAS PURSUING A NEW PASSION: DANCING. AFTER WATCHING FROM THE SIDELINES OF THE ROSELAND, MALCOLM WAS ITCHING TO SWING.

HE PRACTICED EVERY CHANCE AND EVERY PLACE HE COULD. SOON HE WAS READY TO HIT THE FLOOR.

WHEN NEGRO DANCE NIGHT ARRIVED, MALCOLM WAS A SENSATION.

GO, RED, GO!

HE QUICKLY BECAME THE CENTER OF ATTENTION ON THE DANCE FLOOR. EVERYONE WANTED A CHANCE TO LINDY HOP WITH THE YOUNG, RED-HAIRED PLAYER—

—INCLUDING A WHITE WOMAN MALCOLM LATER REFERRED TO AS "SOPHIA."

DESPITE THE SEGREGATION POLICIES AT THE ROSELAND, WHITES WERE ALLOWED TO DANCE ON NEGRO DANCE NIGHTS. ON THOSE NIGHTS, WOMEN LIKE SOPHIA FLOCKED TO THE ROSELAND IN SEARCH OF A TASTE OF BLACK SOCIETY'S "FORBIDDEN FRUITS."

AND SOPHIA HAD SET HER SIGHTS ON MALCOLM.

DECADES LATER, MALCOLM WOULD SAY THAT DROPPING HIS BLACK DANCE PARTNER FOR A WHITE WOMAN WAS A SHAMEFUL EXAMPLE OF HOW LITTLE RESPECT HE HAD FOR HIMSELF AND HIS RACE.

BUT MALCOLM WAS TOO FLATTERED AND INTRIGUED BY THE ATTRACTIVE BLOND WOMAN TO FEEL ASHAMED AT THE TIME.

EVEN THOUGH SOPHIA WAS NOT AS GOOD A DANCER AS MALCOLM'S FORMER PARTNER, SHE WAS WHITE AND GORGEOUS—THE ULTIMATE STATUS SYMBOL AMONG ROXBURY'S HIPSTERS.

MALCOLM AND SOPHIA BECAME AN ITEM. THE TWO WERE CONSTANTLY TOGETHER IN ROXBURY—DINING, DANCING, OR DRIVING AROUND IN SOPHIA'S FINE NEW CADILLAC.

WORD SOON SPREAD THROUGH ROXBURY: YOUNG MALCOLM WAS A KEPT MAN.

HIS SISTER ELLA WAS UPSET BY THE NEWS— SHE WAS ALREADY SUSPICIOUS OF MANY OF MALCOLM'S NEW "FRIENDS," BUT THIS WAS TOO MUCH.

DESPERATE TO SEPARATE HIM FROM THESE BAD INFLUENCES, ELLA ARRANGED FOR 16-YEAR-OLD MALCOLM TO GET A JOB ON THE NEW HAVEN RAILROAD'S BOSTON-TO-NEW YORK YANKEE CLIPPER.

ON THE TRAIN, MALCOLM PUSHED A CART, SELLING SANDWICHES AND OTHER FOOD TO THE PREDOMINANTLY WHITE PASSENGERS.

HE APPROACHED THE JOB WITH CLOWNISH ENTHUSIASM—HE KNEW THAT IF HE ENTERTAINED THE CUSTOMERS AS HE SOLD THEM THEIR MEALS, HIS TIPS WOULD IMPROVE.

AND HE HAD ANOTHER REASON TO BE IN A GOOD MOOD: THE TRAIN'S FINAL DESTINATION AND LAYOVER BEFORE THE RETURN TRIP.

NEW YORK CITY'S HARLEM HAD LONG BEEN A DESTINATION FOR BLACK YOUTH IN SEARCH OF EXCITEMENT. MALCOLM WOULD BE NO EXCEPTION.

AT FIRST, MALCOLM BUSIED HIMSELF VISITING THE LANDMARK ATTRACTIONS HE'D HEARD SO MUCH ABOUT—THE GREAT SAVOY BALLROOM, THE ELEGANT HOTEL THERESA, AND THE FAMOUS NIGHTCLUB AND BAR SMALL'S PARADISE.

WANDERING THE STREETS, HE SAW ANOTHER SIDE OF THE CITY IN FULL AND OPEN VIEW— NEW YORK'S VERSIONS OF THE PIMPS, PUSHERS, AND HUSTLERS THAT USUALLY STUCK TO THE SHADOWS BACK HOME IN ROXBURY.

MALCOLM TOOK IT ALL IN, SENSING HE WAS ON THE BRINK OF HIS NEXT CAREER OPPORTUNITY. HIS SISTER'S PLAN TO GET HIM OUT OF ROXBURY MIGHT HAVE BEEN SOUND, BUT TRANSPORTING HIM TO NEW YORK WAS LIKE LETTING THE FOX INTO THE HENHOUSE.

"ALL OF IT WAS ROXBURY'S WEST END MAGNIFIED A THOUSAND TIMES," MALCOLM LATER SAID. "NEW YORK WAS HEAVEN TO ME!"

MALCOLM ALSO REMEMBERED THAT HARLEM HAD "NARCOTIZED" HIM. THIS WAS TRUE IN A LITERAL AS WELL AS A FIGURATIVE SENSE.

WHILE HE'D ALREADY EXPERIMENTED WITH DRUGS AND ALCOHOL WITH LOCALS IN ROXBURY, IN HARLEM HE WAS HIGH MOST OF HIS WAKING DAY.

IT COULD BE SAID THAT THE MOST DIFFICULT PART OF MALCOLM'S FIRST HARLEM EXPERIENCE WAS THAT HE EVENTUALLY HAD TO RETURN HOME.

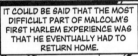

WHETHER HE WAS HIGH, AMBIVALENT ABOUT RETURNING TO ROXBURY, OR SIMPLY TIRED OF PLAYING THE CLOWN FOR WHITE PASSENGERS, MALCOLM SEEMED DIFFERENT NOW.

PASSENGERS BEGAN TO COMPLAIN ABOUT THE WILD YOUNG SANDWICH VENDOR WHOSE INCREASINGLY OUTRAGEOUS BEHAVIOR WAS DISRESPECTFUL TO THE WHITE CUSTOMERS.

MALCOLM SURELY SENSED HIS LUCK WAS RUNNING OUT. HE FULLY LEFT HIS JOB IN 1942 AFTER A YEAR OF ON-AND-OFF EMPLOYMENT...

...USING THE FREE TRAIN-TRAVEL PRIVILEGES HE'D RACKED UP TO RETURN TO LANSING.

AFTER A ROCKY FEW MONTHS WITH HIS FAMILY IN MICHIGAN, THOUGH, HE RETURNED TO HARLEM AND EASILY LANDED ANOTHER RAILROAD JOB.

THE JOB DID NOT LAST LONG. THIS TIME MALCOLM WAS FIRED, NOT FOR RUDENESS TO CUSTOMERS...

...BUT RATHER FOR MINGLING WITH THE WHITE WAITRESSES WHO ALSO WORKED THE TRAIN. THE COMPANY RULES FORBADE BLACK AND WHITE EMPLOYEES TO INTERACT.

ALREADY REJECTED BY HIS FAMILY, WHO WERE SHOCKED BY HIS STREET-HUSTLER MANNER DURING HIS VISIT HOME, MALCOLM FOUND HIMSELF ALONE, UNEMPLOYED, AND ADRIFT IN HARLEM.

IN EARLY 1943, WITH NO PLACE ELSE TO GO, 17-YEAR-OLD MALCOLM RETURNED TO SMALL'S PARADISE.

MALCOLM WOULD SPEND HOURS AT SMALL'S, HOPING TO CATCH A GLIMPSE OF ONE OF THE CELEBRITIES WHO WERE REGULARS.

Y'KNOW, MALCOLM, I HEAR THE BOSS IS LOOKIN' T'HIRE A NEW WAITER...

DIDN'T YOU USED TO WORK THE DINING CAR ON THE NEW HAVEN LINE?

WITH THOSE CREDENTIALS, MALCOLM GOT THE JOB.

AT SMALL'S, MALCOLM WAS A MODEL EMPLOYEE. PERHAPS HE FELT LESS BELITTLED SERVING BLACK HARLEMITES THAN HE DID SERVING WHITE TRAIN PASSENGERS...

...OR PERHAPS IT WAS THE CUSTOMERS THEMSELVES. SMALL'S OLD-TIMERS QUICKLY TOOK MALCOLM UNDER THEIR WING, TELLING HIM STORIES OF HARLEM BEFORE THE DEPRESSION.

THEY TOLD HIM ABOUT THE RENAISSANCE OF THE 1920S, WHEN BLACK ARTISTS THRIVED AND WHITES THRONGED TO HARLEM TO BE ENTERTAINED IN PLACES LIKE THE COTTON CLUB AND THE SAVOY BALLROOM...

...WHEN PROHIBITION SPEAKEASIES FLOURISHED AND JAZZ GREATS PLAYED TILL DAWN...

...POPULARIZING MUSIC THAT PUT HARLEM AT THE CENTER OF THE WORLD MAP OF JAZZ HOT SPOTS.

COTTON CLUB

MALCOLM TOOK IT ALL IN, LEARNING ABOUT HIS CULTURAL HERITAGE THROUGH STORIES OF HARLEM'S PAST.

THEIR WORDS KEPT MEMORIES OF A MORE VITAL BLACK CAPITAL ALIVE. BUT THE OLD-TIMERS HAD MORE TO TEACH.

KNOWING MALCOLM LIKED LISTENING TO THEM, SOME OF THE OLD-TIMERS BEGAN TELLING HIM STORIES OF THEIR OWN EXPLOITS.

SOME WERE MEMBERS OF HARLEM'S LEGENDARY CRIMINAL UNDERGROUND. THEIR STORIES FASCINATED MALCOLM, AND WOULD PROVE INSTRUCTIVE AS WELL.

23

CHAPTER FOUR: *THE HUSTLER LIFE*

A MAN KNOWN AS "FEWCLOTHES" TAUGHT MALCOLM THE TRICKS OF THE PICKPOCKET TRADE.

THE CAT BURGLER "JUMPSTEADY" TOLD MALCOLM HOW HE SUCCESSFULLY ROBBED HOUSES AND FENCED THE STOLEN GOODS.

THE PIMP "DOLLAR BILL" ALWAYS FLASHED A ROLL OF CASH WITH A HUNDRED-DOLLAR BILL ON THE TOP—AND SINGLES BELOW.

"SAMMY THE PIMP" COULD SPOT A POTENTIAL PROSTITUTE JUST BY THE LOOK ON HER FACE.

MALCOLM CONSIDERED THESE MEN TRAGIC EXAMPLES OF EXCEPTIONAL PEOPLE WHO, BECAUSE THEY WERE BLACK IN A WHITE WORLD, HAD NO ALTERNATIVE BUT TO USE THEIR TALENTS TO CRIMINAL ENDS.

BUT HE ALSO SAW THE OPPORTUNITIES THEIR SCHOOLING OFFERED HIM.

THEY INTRODUCED HIM TO THE CURRENT CROP OF PLAYERS, HUSTLERS, THIEVES, CON MEN, PIMPS, AND DRUG DEALERS WHO ALSO VISITED SMALL'S.

THESE NEW ASSOCIATIONS WOULD SERVE MALCOLM WELL IN THE MONTHS TO COME.

HE QUICKLY FOUND A WAY TO GENERATE SOME EXTRA INCOME BY BECOMING A NUMBERS RUNNER.

EVERY DAY IN HARLEM, LEGIONS OF PEOPLE WOULD BET FROM PENNIES TO THOUSANDS OF DOLLARS ON THE LAST THREE DIGITS OF THE RACETRACK'S DAILY TOTAL DOLLAR TAKE.

MALCOLM TOOK BETS, MEMORIZED EACH PLAYER'S NAME AND NUMBERS, AND PAID OFF THE WINNERS FOR A SMALL PERCENTAGE OF THE CASH HANDED IN.

THE PAY WAS GOOD, BUT ALL IT DID WAS GIVE MALCOLM A TASTE FOR MORE.

MALCOLM FOUND THAT IF HE APPROACHED THE HUSTLERS AT SMALL'S WITH THE SAME DEFERENCE AS HIS BEST CUSTOMERS, THEY'D THROW HIM BITS OF ILLICIT WORK...

...AND THE OCCASIONAL STOLEN SUIT—THE BETTER TO ATTRACT NEW BUSINESS.

MALCOLM'S RELATIONSHIP WITH SAMMY THE PIMP WORKED ALONG THESE LINES, TOO. MALCOLM KEPT AN EYE OUT FOR MEN LOOKING FOR FEMALE COMPANY...

...AND IN EXCHANGE FOR TIPS, HE'D DIRECT THEM TO ONE OF SAMMY'S GIRLS WITH THE PROMISE OF A GOOD TIME.

ONE DAY MALCOLM RAN INTO A BLACK SAILOR AT SMALL'S...

YOU OKAY, BROTHER?

YEAH, JUST KINDA SAD. HERE I AM IN HARLEM, AND MY GIRL'S A LONG WAYS AWAY...

MALCOLM KNEW THERE WERE STRICT RULES AGAINST SOLICITING SERVICE- MEN. A BAR COULD LOSE ITS LICENSE IF SOMEONE INSIDE WAS CAUGHT OFFERING TO PROCURE A PROSTITUTE FOR A SAILOR.

EXIT

BUT MALCOLM LIKED LIVING DANGEROUSLY.

BROTHER, YOU NEED A WOMAN NOW! CALL THIS NUMBER—SHE'LL TELL YOU WHERE YOU CAN HOOK UP WITH HER.

THANKS, FRIEND—I'M FEELIN' BETTER ALREADY.

AS THE SAILOR LEFT, MALCOLM STARTED TO FEEL UNEASY. HE WAITED A SHORT TIME BEFORE CALLING THE NUMBER TO CHECK ON THE SAILOR'S ARRIVAL.

SO HE WAS ONLY HALF SURPRISED WHEN...

SORRY, RED— AIN'T HAD NO SAILORS COME CALLIN' TONIGHT.

THE "SAILOR," MALCOLM FIGURED, WAS REALLY AN UNDERCOVER MILITARY POLICEMAN, WHICH MEANT HE WOULD SOON BE IN DEEP TROUBLE.

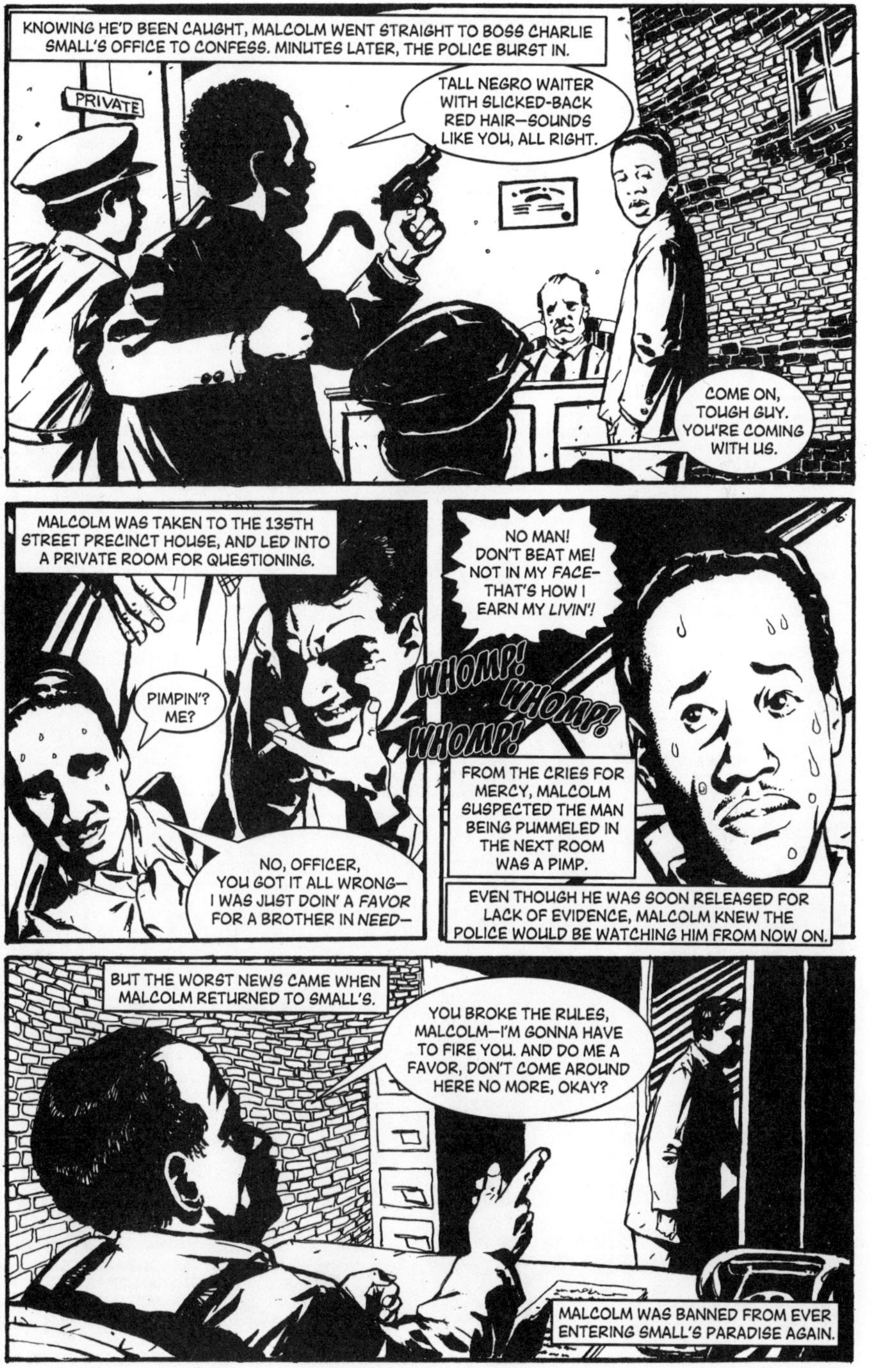
KNOWING HE'D BEEN CAUGHT, MALCOLM WENT STRAIGHT TO BOSS CHARLIE SMALL'S OFFICE TO CONFESS. MINUTES LATER, THE POLICE BURST IN.
PRIVATE
TALL NEGRO WAITER WITH SLICKED-BACK RED HAIR—SOUNDS LIKE YOU, ALL RIGHT.
COME ON, TOUGH GUY. YOU'RE COMING WITH US.
MALCOLM WAS TAKEN TO THE 135TH STREET PRECINCT HOUSE, AND LED INTO A PRIVATE ROOM FOR QUESTIONING.
PIMPIN'? ME?
NO, OFFICER, YOU GOT IT ALL WRONG—I WAS JUST DOIN' A *FAVOR* FOR A BROTHER IN *NEED*—
NO MAN! DON'T BEAT ME! NOT IN MY *FACE*—THAT'S HOW I EARN MY *LIVIN'*!
WHOMP! WHOMP! WHOMP!
FROM THE CRIES FOR MERCY, MALCOLM SUSPECTED THE MAN BEING PUMMELED IN THE NEXT ROOM WAS A PIMP.
EVEN THOUGH HE WAS SOON RELEASED FOR LACK OF EVIDENCE, MALCOLM KNEW THE POLICE WOULD BE WATCHING HIM FROM NOW ON.
BUT THE WORST NEWS CAME WHEN MALCOLM RETURNED TO SMALL'S.
YOU BROKE THE RULES, MALCOLM—I'M GONNA HAVE TO FIRE YOU. AND DO ME A FAVOR, DON'T COME AROUND HERE NO MORE, OKAY?
MALCOLM WAS BANNED FROM EVER ENTERING SMALL'S PARADISE AGAIN.

MALCOLM TURNED TO SAMMY THE PIMP FOR ASSISTANCE.

WAY I SEE IT, SON, BEST THING TO DO NOW IS TO START DEALIN' REEFER.

START WITH YOUR MUSICIAN FRIENDS—THEY REALLY DIG THE WEED!

WITH SAMMY STAKING HIM, MALCOLM WAS IN BUSINESS.

AGAIN, MALCOLM'S FRIENDLY MANNER WORKED TO HIS ADVANTAGE. HE BECAME A TRUSTED DEALER BOTH TO THE MUSICIANS WHOSE WORK HE ADORED AND TO THE REGULAR CUSTOMERS.

SINCE DRUGS WERE NOW ALWAYS ON HAND, HIS PERSONAL USE INCREASED, TOO.

WITH A STEADY STREAM OF CASH COMING IN, MALCOLM COULD AFFORD TO BE HIGH ON EITHER MARIJUANA OR COCAINE MOST OF THE TIME.

ROXBURY

AND WITH A BANKROLL IN HIS POCKET, HE COULD EVEN AFFORD TO TAKE A TRIP TO CATCH UP WITH FAMILY AND FRIENDS.

THE RECEPTION HE RECEIVED FROM HIS SISTER ELLA WAS COLD, AT BEST. HER DISAPPOINTMENT IN HER BROTHER'S LIFESTYLE WAS OBVIOUS.

ALTHOUGH SHE LET HIM STAY IN HER HOME, SHE DID NOT HESITATE TO MAKE CLEAR HER OPINION OF HIM.

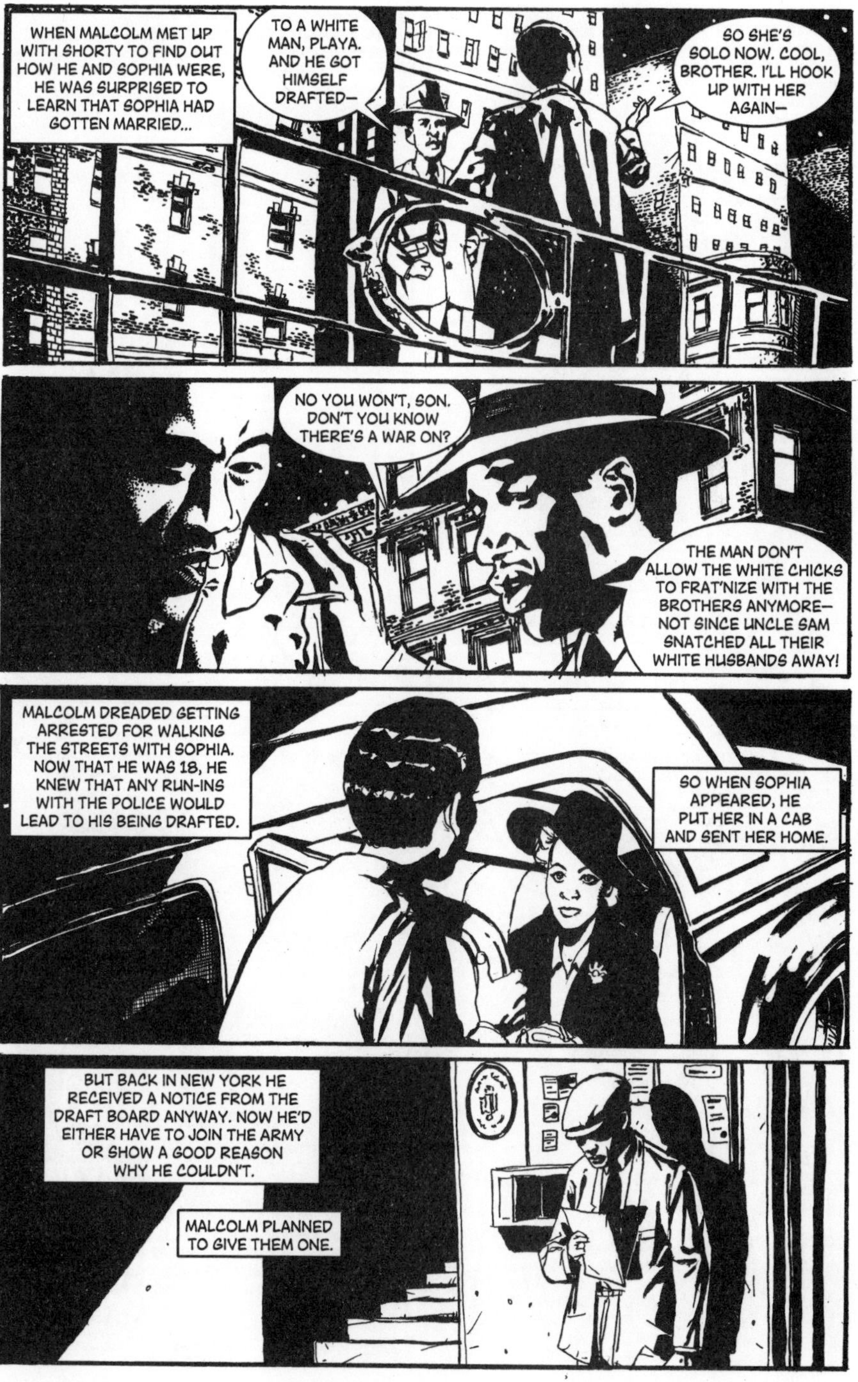
WHEN MALCOLM MET UP WITH SHORTY TO FIND OUT HOW HE AND SOPHIA WERE, HE WAS SURPRISED TO LEARN THAT SOPHIA HAD GOTTEN MARRIED...
TO A WHITE MAN, PLAYA. AND HE GOT HIMSELF DRAFTED—
SO SHE'S SOLO NOW. COOL, BROTHER. I'LL HOOK UP WITH HER AGAIN—
NO YOU WON'T, SON. DON'T YOU KNOW THERE'S A WAR ON?
THE MAN DON'T ALLOW THE WHITE CHICKS TO FRAT'NIZE WITH THE BROTHERS ANYMORE— NOT SINCE UNCLE SAM SNATCHED ALL THEIR WHITE HUSBANDS AWAY!
MALCOLM DREADED GETTING ARRESTED FOR WALKING THE STREETS WITH SOPHIA. NOW THAT HE WAS 18, HE KNEW THAT ANY RUN-INS WITH THE POLICE WOULD LEAD TO HIS BEING DRAFTED.
SO WHEN SOPHIA APPEARED, HE PUT HER IN A CAB AND SENT HER HOME.
BUT BACK IN NEW YORK HE RECEIVED A NOTICE FROM THE DRAFT BOARD ANYWAY. NOW HE'D EITHER HAVE TO JOIN THE ARMY OR SHOW A GOOD REASON WHY HE COULDN'T.
MALCOLM PLANNED TO GIVE THEM ONE.

THE NEXT DAY, MALCOLM DECLARED HIS MILITARY INTENTIONS TO ANYONE ON THE STREET WHO WOULD LISTEN.

OH, MAN, I'M FRANTIC TO JOIN—THE *JAPANESE* ARMY!

HE SUSPECTED THAT MILITARY SPIES WERE PATROLLING THE STREETS OF HARLEM, AND HOPED THAT HIS ERRATIC BEHAVIOR WOULD GIVE THEM SOMETHING TO REPORT.

MALCOLM WAS REQUIRED TO REPORT TO HIS LOCAL DRAFT BOARD. HE DID—IN OVER-THE-TOP STYLE.

CRAZY-O, DADDY-O, GET ME MOVING! I CAN'T WAIT!

AS HE STOOD ON LINE FOR HIS PHYSICAL EXAM, HE SHOOK UNCONTROLLABLY AND REFUSED TO KEEP QUIET.

I'M GONNA FIGHT ON ALL FRONTS, GONNA BE A *GENERAL*, MAN—

BUT MALCOLM SAVED HIS BEST SHOTS FOR LAST. WHEN THE ARMY PSYCHIATRIST INTERVIEWED HIM...

WANT TO GET SENT DOWN SOUTH. ORGANIZE THEM NIGGER SOLDIERS, YOU DIG?

STEAL US SOME GUNS AND KILL US SOME CRACKERS!

MALCOLM'S 4-F CARD ARRIVED IN THE MAIL A FEW DAYS LATER. JUST AS HE'D HOPED, HE WAS JUDGED PSYCHOLOGICALLY UNFIT FOR SERVICE.

CHAPTER FIVE: *A DOWNWARD SPIRAL*

NOT HAVING TO SERVE IN THE ARMY WAS ONE WEIGHT OFF MALCOLM'S SHOULDERS. BUT OTHER WEIGHTS WERE GETTING HEAVIER.

NARCOTICS DETECTIVES IN HARLEM HAD BEGUN TO TAKE NOTICE OF MALCOLM'S DRUG DEALING.

SINCE THE POLICE NEEDED TO FIND DRUGS ON A SUSPECT TO ARREST HIM, MALCOLM HAD VARIOUS METHODS TO DISPOSE OF DRUGS IN A HURRY.

WHENEVER HE THOUGHT HE SAW A DETECTIVE, HE'D DUMP HIS SUPPLY BEFORE THE POLICE COULD FRISK HIM.

MALCOLM DISCOVERED THAT THE FRUSTRATED POLICE HAD PLACED HIM ON A SPECIAL HARASSMENT HIT LIST.

THEY BROKE IN AND SEARCHED MALCOLM'S APARTMENT. EVEN THOUGH MALCOLM NEVER KEPT DRUGS AT HOME, HE FEARED THE COPS WOULD PLANT DRUGS THERE, SO HE WAS FORCED TO MOVE.

BETWEEN POLICE SURVEILLANCE AND MALCOLM'S OWN DRUG-INDUCED PARANOIA, HE WAS SOON THROWING AWAY MORE DRUGS THAN HE WAS SELLING.

ADD TO THIS THE COST OF HIS MOUNTING GAMBLING DEBTS, AND MALCOLM CLEARLY NEEDED A NEW LINE OF WORK.

BY 1944, MALCOLM, ONCE AGAIN WITH THE AID OF SAMMY THE PIMP, GRADUATED TO THE NEXT LEVEL OF THE HUSTLE: ARMED ROBBERY.

A SERIES OF SUCCESSFUL STICKUPS MADE MALCOLM FINANCIALLY FLUSH AGAIN, BUT THE RISKS COULDN'T HAVE BEEN HIGHER.

THE SOUND OF SIRENS USUALLY DROVE CHILLS UP MALCOLM'S SPINE AND SENT HIM AND SAMMY RUNNING.

BUT ON ONE OCCASION, MALCOLM DECIDED THAT FLEEING THE SCENE OF THE CRIME WASN'T NECESSARILY THE BEST ESCAPE ROUTE.

YOU FLAGGIN' DOWN THE COPS? THEY'LL TAKE US IN!!

BE COOL, SAMMY. I GOT AN IDEA THAT'LL THROW 'EM OFF.

EXCUSE ME, OFFICER. CAN YOU TELL US HOW TO GET TO ST. NICHOLAS AVENUE?

IS THAT WHY YOU STOPPED US?! FOR DIRECTIONS?! DAMN IT, BOY, WE GOT JOBS TO DO!

AS MALCOLM LATER SAID, WHITE COPS WERE SO CONFIDENT OF THEIR SUPERIOR INTELLIGENCE THAT THEY NEVER CONSIDERED THAT A NEGRO COULD HUSTLE THEM.

MAN, MALCOLM— YOU ARE ONE COOL GAMBLER!

MALCOLM'S LUCK GAMBLING WITH HIS FREEDOM, HOWEVER, WAS BETTER THAN HIS LUCK GAMBLING ON THE NUMBERS...

"WEST INDIAN ARCHIE," A LEGENDARY BOOKIE, HAD A BONE TO PICK WITH MALCOLM. HE SAID MALCOLM HAD LIED ABOUT A NUMBER AND TAKEN $300 FROM HIM.

BREAKING INTO MALCOLM'S APARTMENT, HE MADE HIS DEMANDS CRYSTAL CLEAR.

YOU GOT UNTIL MIDNIGHT TOMORROW TO PAY ME.

ARCHIE WAS ONE OF THE MOST ESTABLISHED AND RESPECTED BOOKIES IN HARLEM. HE HAD A PHOTOGRAPHIC MEMORY AND KEPT THOUSANDS OF BETS IN HIS HEAD.

ARCHIE WAS ALSO OLD, AND MALCOLM THOUGHT HIS MEMORY WAS FAILING. BUT MALCOLM KNEW THAT ARCHIE WOULD NEVER BACK DOWN, SO HE STARTED CARRYING A GUN FOR PROTECTION.

WORD OF ARCHIE'S THREAT SPREAD QUICKLY. THE NEXT DAY MALCOLM FELT LIKE A MARKED MAN. PEOPLE AVOIDED HIM. NO ONE ASKED IF HE HAD ANY REEFER OR WAS RUNNING BETS.

IT WAS CLEAR THAT THE PUBLIC HAD SIDED WITH ARCHIE.

SO THAT EVENING, WHEN ARCHIE BURST INTO A LOCAL BAR AND GOT THE DROP ON MALCOLM, NOBODY INTERFERED.

MALCOLM CONSIDERED MAKING A PLAY FOR HIS GUN WHEN...

YOU'RE THINKING YOU CAN KILL ME FIRST, MALCOLM. KILL ME, YOU'VE LOST ANYWAY. ALL YOU CAN DO IS GO TO PRISON.

AFTER A FEW TENSE MOMENTS, ONE OF ARCHIE'S FRIENDS APPROACHED TO BREAK THE STANDOFF.

SLOWLY, CAREFULLY, MALCOLM LEFT THE BAR.

NO ONE SAID A WORD, BUT EVERY-ONE SAW WHAT HAD HAPPENED. IN MALCOLM'S RECOLLECTIONS, THIS MOMENT OF SUBMISSION PACKED A LESSON THAT ECHOED THROUGHOUT HIS LIFE: HE WHO BACKS DOWN IS DONE FOR.

IN THE BLINK OF AN EYE, MALCOLM'S HARLEM HUSTLING DAYS WERE OVER. HE HAD LOST FACE, AND WITH IT THE RESPECT OF HIS FELLOW HUSTLERS.

MENS

WITHOUT THIS, MALCOLM KNEW HE WAS DOOMED. ARCHIE, OTHER RIVAL HUSTLERS, THE COPS... THEY WERE ALL AFTER MALCOLM NOW. IT WAS ONLY A MATTER OF TIME.

ALL OPTIONS GONE, MALCOLM CHOSE TO DROWN HIS SORROWS WITH DRUGS AND WANDER THE HARLEM STREETS, ANONYMOUS AND ALONE.

BUT HE STILL HAD ONE FRIEND LEFT IN NEW YORK— SAMMY THE PIMP, WHO MADE A FEW PHONE CALLS TO BOSTON.

HOMEBOY!

SHORTY?!?!

MALCOLM'S ROXBURY FRIEND SHORTY HAD DRIVEN ALL NIGHT TO COME TO HIS RESCUE.

WE'LL STOP AT YOUR PLACE, PACK, AND THEN HEAD BACK HOME, OKAY?

EVEN THOUGH HARLEM WAS CLOSED TO MALCOLM, SHORTY GAVE HIM HOPE THAT HIS HUSTLING DAYS WERE NOT QUITE OVER.

34

BACK IN ROXBURY, MALCOLM'S FIRST STOP WAS TO VISIT ELLA. SHE WAS JUST AS DISENCHANTED WITH HIM AS EVER.

THE LAST TIME HE'D VISITED, HE WAS ALREADY DEEP INTO THE ROBBERY HUSTLE AND HAD USED HIS SKILLS TO STEAL HIS AUNT GRACE'S FUR COAT.

WHEN SHE FOUND OUT, ELLA WAS INCENSED, AND FIGURED THE ONLY WAY TO TEACH MALCOLM A LESSON WAS TO CALL THE POLICE ON HIM.

MALCOLM WAS ARRESTED IN BOSTON, CONVICTED OF LARCENY, AND GIVEN A SUSPENDED SENTENCE.

NOW ELLA COULD SEE THAT HER EFFORTS HAD FAILED AGAIN.

HER BROTHER HAD ONLY GROWN MORE DESPERATE.

HAVING PAID HIS RESPECTS TO HIS SISTER AND GOTTEN HIS FAMILY COMMITMENTS OUT OF THE WAY, MALCOLM'S SECOND VISIT WAS WITH A LOCAL COCAINE DEALER.

MUCH AS HE MIGHT HAVE DENIED IT TO HIMSELF, HE WAS HOOKED ON COCAINE AND NEEDED TO GET HIMSELF "FIXED UP" JUST TO THINK CLEARLY.

CHAPTER SIX: ONE LAST HUSTLE

WITH HIS THINKING PRECARIOUSLY INFLUENCED BY DRUGS, MALCOLM MOVED IN WITH SHORTY.

HE SPENT THE NEXT MONTH IN THE HOUSE "LAYING DEAD," BUT USUALLY WAS EITHER SLEEPING...OR PLANNING HIS NEXT MOVE.

BY THE TIME HE EMERGED TO RECONNECT WITH HIS ROXBURY FRIENDS, A PLAN HAD ALREADY TAKEN SHAPE IN HIS MIND.

SHORTY INTRODUCED HIM TO HIS FRIEND RUDY, A YOUNG HALF ITALIAN, HALF BLACK WHO WORKED AS A WAITER AT PRIVATE PARTIES HELD IN THE HOMES OF THE RICH.

BY THIS TIME IN 1945 THE WAR WAS OVER AND THE TROOPS HAD RETURNED HOME. BUT SOPHIA'S HUSBAND HAD TAKEN A JOB THAT SENT HIM AWAY ON BUSINESS...

...SO SHE AND MALCOLM WERE REUNITED AT LAST.

SOPHIA GAVE HIM MONEY TO BUY MORE DRUGS AND TO SERVE AS A FINANCIAL STAKE IN MALCOLM'S NEXT HUSTLE.

SHE ALSO INTRODUCED MALCOLM TO HER SISTER, WHO SHARED SOPHIA'S TASTES IN RISKY ENTERTAINMENT AND MEN.

MALCOLM REVEALED HIS PLAN: THE GANG WOULD SPECIALIZE IN "RESIDENCE BURGLARIES."

ALTHOUGH THE OTHERS WERE FASCINATED BY MALCOLM'S SCHEME, MOST OF THEM HADN'T TRIED ANY CRIMINAL ACTIVITIES, LET ALONE SOMETHING AS RISKY AS BREAKING AND ENTERING PRIVATE HOMES.

IT WAS PERHAPS A MEASURE OF MALCOLM'S DESPERATION THAT THIS DIDN'T STOP HIM FROM GOING FORWARD WITH HIS PLAN.

INSTEAD, HE FOUND A USE FOR EACH MEMBER OF THE CREW.

SERVING FOOD AND DRINK IN THE HOMES OF THE RICH WOULD MAKE RUDY AN EXCELLENT "FINDER."

THE GIRLS, BEING ATTRACTIVE AND WHITE, WOULD GET INVITED TO—OR SIMPLY CRASH—PARTIES IN WHITE NEIGHBORHOODS AND CASE THE HOMES FOR ITEMS OF VALUE.

MALCOLM AND SHORTY WOULD PERFORM THE ACTUAL BURGLARIES.

THE GROUP THOUGHT OF IT AS A GAME. ONLY MALCOLM AND SHORTY KNEW HOW SERIOUS IT REALLY WAS.

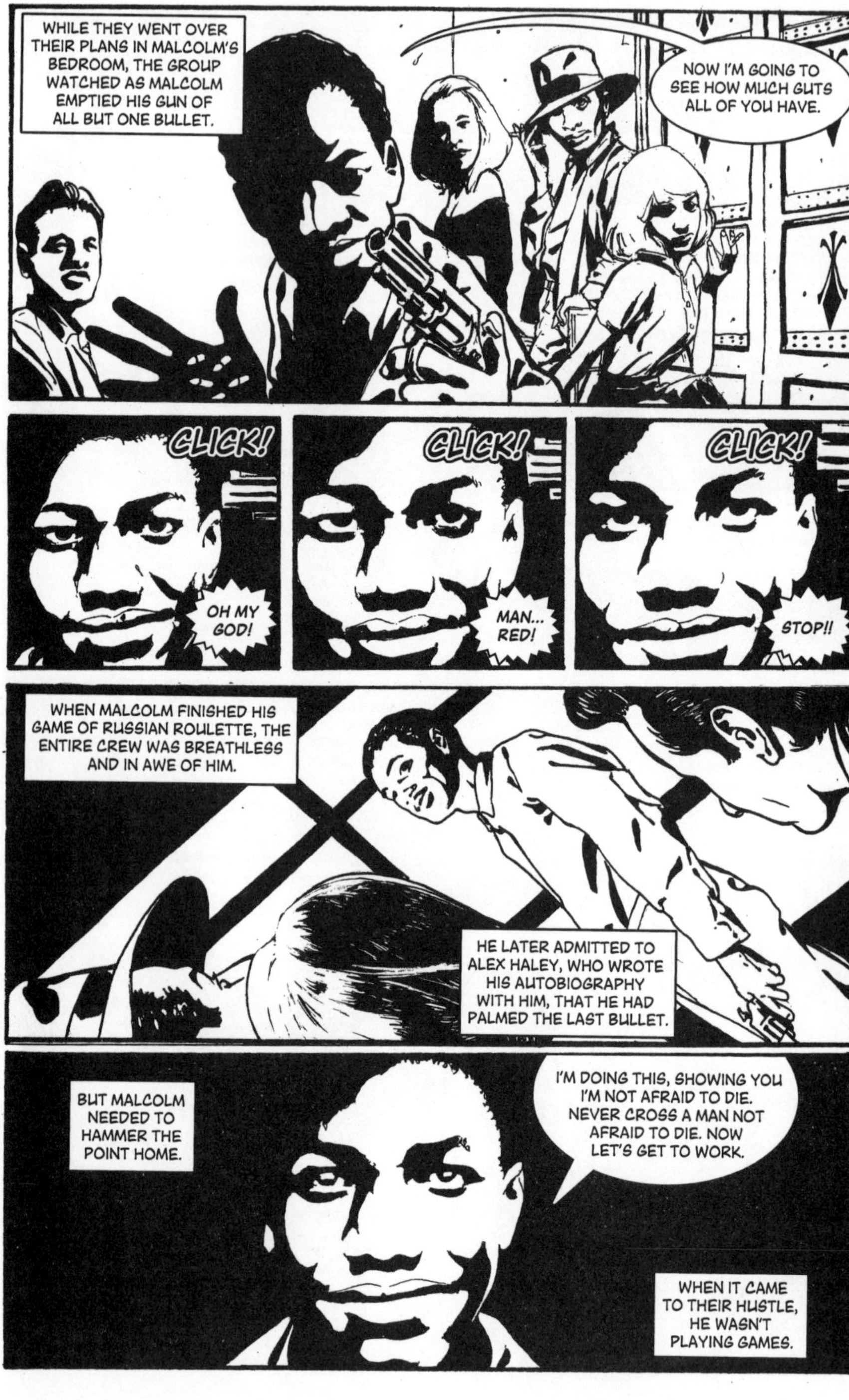
WHILE THEY WENT OVER THEIR PLANS IN MALCOLM'S BEDROOM, THE GROUP WATCHED AS MALCOLM EMPTIED HIS GUN OF ALL BUT ONE BULLET.
NOW I'M GOING TO SEE HOW MUCH GUTS ALL OF YOU HAVE.
CLICK!
OH MY GOD!
CLICK!
MAN... RED!
CLICK!
STOP!!
WHEN MALCOLM FINISHED HIS GAME OF RUSSIAN ROULETTE, THE ENTIRE CREW WAS BREATHLESS AND IN AWE OF HIM.
HE LATER ADMITTED TO ALEX HALEY, WHO WROTE HIS AUTOBIOGRAPHY WITH HIM, THAT HE HAD PALMED THE LAST BULLET.
BUT MALCOLM NEEDED TO HAMMER THE POINT HOME.
I'M DOING THIS, SHOWING YOU I'M NOT AFRAID TO DIE. NEVER CROSS A MAN NOT AFRAID TO DIE. NOW LET'S GET TO WORK.
WHEN IT CAME TO THEIR HUSTLE, HE WASN'T PLAYING GAMES.

AT FIRST, THE GROUP PLAYED ALL THEIR HEISTS BY MALCOLM'S BOOK. BUT BY CHRISTMAS, SUCCESS HAD GONE TO THEIR HEADS.

WITH MALCOLM'S APPROVAL, THEY DISCARDED THE CAREFULLY ESTABLISHED PREPLANNING STAGE, OPTING INSTEAD TO GO ON A STEALING SPREE.

SOPHIA AND HER SISTER WOULD POINT OUT A HOUSE OWNED BY ESPECIALLY RICH PEOPLE.

LEAVING THE MEN IN THE CAR, THE GIRLS WOULD RING THE DOORBELL.

IF SOMEONE ANSWERED, THE GROUP WOULD MOVE ON TO THE NEXT HOUSE.

IF NO ONE WAS HOME, THEY'D BREAK IN AND STEAL ANYTHING NOT NAILED DOWN.

AFTER A WEEK OF RECORD-BREAKING THEFTS, THE ENTIRE GROUP DECIDED TO LIE LOW FOR A WHILE.

MALCOLM FENCED THEIR LOOT, AND THEY SPENT MOST OF THE CASH ON A WEEK OF DRINKING, DRUGS, DANCING, AND SEX.

AS A REWARD FOR HIS GOOD WORK, MALCOLM DECIDED TO KEEP ONE OF THE STOLEN WATCHES FOR HIMSELF.

BY KEEPING HIS ILL-GOTTEN GAINS, MALCOLM WAS BREAKING THE BURGLAR'S CARDINAL RULE: FENCE EVERYTHING YOU STEAL.

BUT THE WATCH WASN'T KEEPING TIME. MALCOLM TOOK IT TO A LOCAL JEWELER TO BE REPAIRED.

SINCE IT WAS TOO COSTLY A WATCH TO BE WORN BY THE TYPICAL ROXBURY RESIDENT, THE JEWELER SUSPECTED IT WAS STOLEN AND INFORMED THE POLICE.

WHEN MALCOLM RETURNED TO THE JEWELER'S TO PICK UP THE REPAIRED WATCH, THE POLICE WERE WAITING FOR HIM.

THEY ASKED HIM TO STEP INTO THE BACK OF THE STORE, BUT INSTEAD, MALCOLM RAISED HIS HANDS AND STOOD PERFECTLY STILL.

I HAVE A GUN UNDER MY JACKET. COULD YOU TAKE IT FROM ME, PLEASE?

MALCOLM KNEW THAT HE WAS IN DEEP TROUBLE. BUT HE HOPED THAT BY GIVING UP HIS WEAPON AND AVOIDING A SHOOT-OUT HE MIGHT BE TREATED MORE LENIENTLY BY THE JUDGE.

IT HARDLY MATTERED. WHILE MALCOLM BELIEVED THAT GIVING UP HIS GUN SAVED HIM FROM GETTING BEATEN BY HIS INTERROGATORS, ALL HOPES OF LENIENCY WERE DASHED WHEN THE POLICE ROUNDED UP THE OTHER SUSPECTS.

THE JUDGE, THE JURY, THE CLERKS, THE BAILIFFS, EVEN MALCOLM'S OWN COURT-APPOINTED LAWYERS WERE APPALLED TO SEE WHITE WOMEN BEING LURED INTO CRIME BY BLACK MEN.

YOU HAD NO BUSINESS MESSING AROUND WITH WHITE GIRLS!

THE VERDICTS CAME DOWN IN FEBRUARY 1946: GUILTY. THE GIRLS WERE SENTENCED TO ONE TO FIVE YEARS AT MASSACHUSETTS WOMEN'S REFORMATORY...

SHORTY WAS SENTENCED TO FOUR CONCURRENT EIGHT-TO-TEN-YEAR TERMS.

AND MALCOLM, NOT YET 21 YEARS OLD, WAS SENTENCED TWICE FOR COMMITTING BURGLARIES IN TWO COUNTIES. HE RECEIVED FOUR CONCURRENT EIGHT-TO-TEN-YEAR TERMS AND THREE CONCURRENT SIX-TO-EIGHT-YEAR TERMS.

OHHH-HHHII

41

AT THE STATE PRISON IN CHARLESTOWN, MALCOLM QUICKLY EARNED A REPUTATION AS AN UNCOOPERATIVE, ANGRY INMATE.

HE'D CURSE THE GUARDS AS THEY PASSED HIS CELL, AND FIGHT WITH OTHER INMATES WHENEVER POSSIBLE.

TALK OF RELIGION ESPECIALLY ENRAGED MALCOLM. PRISON AUTHORITIES FELT RELIGIOUS CONVICTIONS ENCOURAGED REHABILITATION, BUT MALCOLM WANTED NO PART OF IT.

ANGRY EXPLETIVES WOULD ERUPT FROM HIS MOUTH WHENEVER GOD WAS MENTIONED.

HOLY BIBLE

INMATES SOON GAVE MALCOLM THE NICKNAME "SATAN."

FOR HIS OBSCENE SPEECH AND VIOLENT BEHAVIOR, THE GUARDS OFTEN PUT MALCOLM IN SOLITARY CONFINEMENT.

THAT SUITED MALCOLM FINE.

HE PREFERRED PACING HIS CELL UNWATCHED, AND YELLING PROFANITIES IN PRIVATE.

IN TRUTH, SCREAMING IN RAGE AT THE WORLD WAS ALL THAT WAS LEFT FOR HIM TO DO.

AS MALCOLM LATER RECALLED, HE HAD FINALLY HIT BOTTOM.

ALTHOUGH MALCOLM HAD GIVEN UP ON THE WORLD, HIS FAMILY HAD NOT GIVEN UP ON HIM. HIS BROTHER PHILBERT WROTE TO TELL HIM GOD OFFERED A SOLUTION.

MALCOLM REJECTED BOTH HIS BROTHER AND GOD.

HIS BROTHER REGINALD WROTE A SHORT TIME LATER. THIS TIME MALCOLM WAS INTRIGUED.

MUST BE SOME KIND OF HYPE— I'LL DO IT!

HIS SISTER ELLA PETITIONED THE PRISON BOARD TO HAVE HER BROTHER TRANSFERRED OUT OF THE HARSH CHARLESTOWN PRISON AND INTO THE PROGRESSIVE NORFOLK, MASSACHUSETTS, PRISON COLONY.

ELLA KNEW THAT NORFOLK OFFERED MALCOLM HIS BEST CHANCE FOR REHABILITATION. AND MALCOLM HIMSELF HAD SHOWN INTEREST IN NORFOLK'S EXTENSIVE LIBRARY.

IN MARCH 1948, MALCOLM'S TRANSFER WAS GRANTED.

COMPARED TO CHARLESTOWN, NORFOLK WAS A PARADISE. IT HAD TOILETS THAT FLUSHED, PRIVATE ROOMS FOR INMATES, AND EDUCATIONAL REHABILITATION PROGRAMS.

SOON AFTER MALCOLM SETTLED IN, REGINALD PAID HIM A VISIT. MALCOLM WAS ANXIOUS TO HEAR HOW REGINALD'S "NO PORK" PLAN WAS GOING TO GET HIM RELEASED.

INSTEAD, REGINALD REVEALED THAT HIS "HYPE" WAS PART OF A PLAN TO INTRODUCE MALCOLM TO SOMETHING FAR MORE IMPORTANT THAN MERE FREEDOM FROM PRISON.

REGINALD SAID THAT HE, BROTHER PHILBERT, AND SISTER HILDA HAD ALL BECOME BELIEVERS IN THE TEACHINGS OF THE HONORABLE ELIJAH MUHAMMAD, LEADER OF THE NATION OF ISLAM.

LIKE THEIR FATHER BEFORE THEM, THEY HAD BECOME MEMBERS OF A RELIGIOUS ORGANIZATION WITH A BLACK SEPARATIST CREED.

AT FIRST, MALCOLM WAS SKEPTICAL. TO HIM, ORGANIZED RELIGION WAS JUST A METHOD TO SUPPRESS THE BLACK MAN. BUT REGINALD INSISTED THAT THE NATION WAS DIFFERENT IN A FUNDAMENTAL WAY.

GOD IS ALLAH AND ALLAH IS A MAN— A *BLACK* MAN!

BUT THE DEVIL IS ALSO A MAN— A *WHITE* MAN!

MALCOLM RECALLED ALL THE WHITE PEOPLE HE'D KNOWN.

IN ONE WAY OR ANOTHER, HE FELT THEY ALL USED BLACKS TO BETTER THEIR OWN LIVES...

...LEAVING BLACKS LIVING UNDER THE SAME OR WORSE CONDITIONS AS BEFORE.

REGINALD EXPLAINED THAT HISTORY ITSELF HAD BEEN REWRITTEN BY THE WHITE DEVIL TO ELIMINATE THE GLORY OF THE BLACK MAN'S ACCOMPLISHMENTS.

THE WHITE DEVIL HAS HIDDEN FROM YOU THAT OUR PEOPLE DESCEND FROM ANCIENT CIVILIZATIONS RICH IN GOLD AND KINGS.

YOU DON'T EVEN KNOW YOUR TRUE FAMILY NAME! YOU WOULDN'T RECOGNIZE YOUR TRUE LANGUAGE IF YOU HEARD IT!

YOU HAVE BEEN A VICTIM OF THE EVIL OF THE DEVIL WHITE MAN EVER SINCE HE MURDERED AND RAPED AND STOLE YOU FROM YOUR NATIVE LAND.

EVEN THE WHITE DEVIL'S CHRISTIAN GOD WAS WHITE, TO REENFORCE THE BLACK MAN'S INFERIOR STATUS.

CONVERSION TO ISLAM WAS THE ONLY WAY FOR THE BLACK MAN TO SHAKE OFF THE WHITE DEVIL'S CHAINS.

AND TRUE KNOWLEDGE OF THE BLACK MAN COULD BE LEARNED ONLY FROM THE MESSENGER, THE HONORABLE ELIJAH MUHAMMAD.

WHEN REGINALD FINISHED, MALCOLM WAS ANXIOUS TO TAKE THE NEXT STEP TOWARD THE NATION OF ISLAM. WEEKS LATER, HIS SISTER HILDA ARRIVED TO HELP.

Yacub's Tale

THE LOST-FOUND NATION OF ISLAM WAS CREATED BY WALLACE DODD FARD, A TRAVELING SILK SALESMAN. LITTLE IS KNOWN OF FARD. HIS BIRTH DATE, COUNTRY OF ORIGIN, RACE, AND EVEN HIS LEGAL NAME ARE UNCERTAIN.

BUT IN 1930 HE APPEARED IN DETROIT AND SOON AFTER OPENED THE FIRST NATION OF ISLAM TEMPLE THERE.

FARD'S VERSION OF ISLAM BORE LITTLE RESEMBLANCE TO THE TRADITIONAL FAITH. AT ITS CORE WAS THE STORY OF YACUB, THE BLACK SCIENTIST RESPONSIBLE FOR THE CREATION OF THE WHITE RACE.

YACUB, BORN 6,600 YEARS AGO, WAS ONE OF THE "ORIGINAL" HUMANS, ALL OF WHOM WERE BLACK. HIGHLY INTELLIGENT, YACUB HAD A LARGE HEAD, AND AS HE AGED HE CAME TO BE KNOWN AS "THE BIG-HEAD SCIENTIST."

BY AGE 18, YACUB WAS SO SMART THAT HE'D LEARNED HOW TO BREED RACES SCIENTIFICALLY. FOR THIS, HE AND 59,999 OF HIS FOLLOWERS WERE EXILED TO THE ISLAND OF PATMOS.

ANGERED BY HIS REJECTION, "BIG HEAD" DECIDED TO GET HIS REVENGE BY CREATING "A DEVIL RACE—A BLEACHED OUT, WHITE RACE OF PEOPLE."

FROM HIS 59,999 FOLLOWERS YACUB SELECTED THE LIGHTEST-SKINNED CHILDREN AND CROSSBRED THEM. ALTHOUGH YACUB DIED AT THE AGE OF 152, HIS GRAND EXPERIMENT CONTINUED.

EVERY 200 YEARS WOULD YIELD A LIGHTER-SKINNED RACE: FIRST THE "RED RACE," THEN THE "YELLOW RACE," AND, FINALLY, THE "WHITE RACE," ALL DERIVED FROM THE ORIGINAL "BLACK RACE."

46

WHEN THE WHITE DEVIL RACE RETURNED TO THE MAINLAND, IT TOOK THEM ONLY SIX MONTHS TO CREATE HAVOC IN WHAT WAS ONCE A HEAVEN ON EARTH.

THE ORIGINAL BLACK PEOPLE CAPTURED THE WHITE DEVILS, CHAINED THEM, AND SENT THEM TO THE CAVES OF EUROPE.

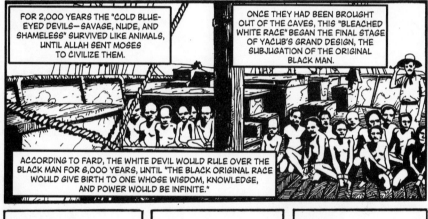

FOR 2,000 YEARS THE "COLD BLUE-EYED DEVILS— SAVAGE, NUDE, AND SHAMELESS" SURVIVED LIKE ANIMALS, UNTIL ALLAH SENT MOSES TO CIVILIZE THEM.

ONCE THEY HAD BEEN BROUGHT OUT OF THE CAVES, THIS "BLEACHED WHITE RACE" BEGAN THE FINAL STAGE OF YACUB'S GRAND DESIGN, THE SUBJUGATION OF THE ORIGINAL BLACK MAN.

ACCORDING TO FARD, THE WHITE DEVIL WOULD RULE OVER THE BLACK MAN FOR 6,000 YEARS, UNTIL "THE BLACK ORIGINAL RACE WOULD GIVE BIRTH TO ONE WHOSE WISDOM, KNOWLEDGE, AND POWER WOULD BE INFINITE."

THAT MAN, ACCORDING TO ELIJAH MUHAMMAD, WAS HIS MENTOR, NATION OF ISLAM FOUNDER WALLACE FARD MUHAMMAD.

ALTHOUGH HE MYSTERIOUSLY DISAPPEARED IN 1934, FARD LEFT BEHIND A GROWING FLOCK OF BLACK BELIEVERS AND A CULTURAL AND RACIAL IDENTITY DENIED THEM IN AMERICA.

YEARS LATER, MALCOLM, LIKE MOST MIDDLE-EASTERN MUSLIMS, WOULD QUESTION THE AUTHENTICITY OF THE YACUB STORY...

...BUT WHEN HILDA FIRST TOLD HIM OF YACUB, MALCOLM, LIKE MANY OTHER ALIENATED YOUNG BLACKS, WAS READY TO BELIEVE.

HE WROTE ELIJAH MUHAMMAD TO TELL HIM OF THE REVELATIONS HILDA HAD JUST PASSED ON TO HIM. HE WANTED THE MESSENGER TO KNOW MALCOLM LITTLE WAS READY TO RECEIVE HIS MESSAGE.

DAYS LATER, MUHAMMAD REPLIED. HE WROTE THAT BEFORE ONE CAN ENTER THE NOI, HE MUST ATONE FOR HIS CRIMINAL PAST AND SUBMIT TO ALLAH BY KNEELING IN PRAYER.

THROUGHOUT MALCOLM'S LIFE, HE'D MADE A POINT OF NEVER BOWING DOWN TO ANYONE. NOW HIS SUBMISSION WAS DEMANDED.

IT TOOK HIM A WEEK, MALCOLM REMEMBERED. EVERY TIME HE BEGAN TO KNEEL, SOMETHING INSIDE MADE HIM STAND BACK UP.

BUT IN THE END, HE DID IT. NOW IT WAS TIME FOR HIM TO MAKE AMENDS FOR HIS EVIL PAST.

HE WROTE LETTERS TO HIS OLD CRIMINAL FRIENDS, OFFERING THEM REDEMPTION IF THEY EMBRACED ISLAM, ALLAH, AND ELIJAH MUHAMMAD.

HE EVEN WROTE TO PRESIDENT TRUMAN TO TELL HIM THAT THE WHITE DEVIL WAS RESPONSIBLE FOR THE BLACK MAN'S SORRY CONDITION.

HE RECEIVED NO REPLIES.

DESPITE HAVING EARNED ELIJAH MUHAMMAD'S BLESSING TO ENTER THE NATION OF ISLAM, MALCOLM WAS TROUBLED.

HE BELIEVED HIS DAILY LETTERS TO MUHAMMAD REVEALED ONLY THE LIMITATIONS OF HIS INTELLIGENCE. HIS FAILED ATTEMPTS TO SPREAD THE WORD OF THE NOI SIMPLY CONFIRMED IT.

WITH HIS LIMITED VOCABULARY AND POOR PENMANSHIP, MALCOLM WAS UNLIKELY TO BE AN ASSET TO THE NOI.

THE REALIZATION ANGERED HIM. HE'D WASTED YEARS OF HIS LIFE...AND THE WHITE DEVIL WAS TO BLAME.

FROM THE EIGHTH-GRADE TEACHER WHO DISCOURAGED HIS AMBITIONS, TO THE DEALERS WHO PLIED HIM WITH DRUGS...

...THEY ALL KEPT MALCOLM FROM THE EDUCATION HE NEEDED TO SPREAD NEWS OF THE MESSENGER.

KNOWLEDGE WAS THE AMMUNITION MALCOLM NEEDED TO FIGHT THE BATTLE THAT WAS BEGINNING TO TAKE SHAPE IN HIS MIND.

HE DOUBLED HIS RESOLVE TO USE THE PRISON'S LIBRARY TO GIVE HIM THE EDUCATION WHITE SOCIETY HAD DENIED HIM.

HE BEGAN BY COPYING OUT EVERY WORD IN THE DICTIONARY, STARTING WITH THE LETTER "A," UNTIL HE KNEW THEIR DEFINITIONS AND HOW TO WRITE THEM CLEARLY.

"MY ALMA MATER WAS BOOKS..."

...AND MALCOLM READ HUNDREDS OF THEM. THE LIBRARY CONTAINED A WEALTH OF BOOKS ABOUT HISTORY AND RELIGION, TWO SUBJECTS FOR WHICH MALCOLM WAS PARTICULARLY HUNGRY.

MALCOLM READ MORNING AND NIGHT—BY HIS OWN ACCOUNT, MORE THAN 15 HOURS A DAY. AFTER LIGHTS OUT, HE'D SIT ON HIS CELL FLOOR AND READ BY THE LIGHT OF THE BULB DOWN THE HALL.

EVERY 58 MINUTES, MALCOLM WOULD HOP INTO BED AND FEIGN SLEEP UNTIL THE GUARD ON ROUNDS PASSED HIS CELL.

AS HIS KNOWLEDGE OF HISTORY GREW, MALCOLM BELIEVED IT BORE OUT ELIJAH MUHAMMAD'S TEACHINGS OF THE BLACK MAN'S GLORIOUS PAST.

IN THE LETTERS HE CONTINUED TO WRITE, MALCOLM BEGAN TO ADD HIS OWN SUPPORTING ARGUMENTS INSTEAD OF SIMPLY AGREEING WITH MUHAMMAD'S LESSONS.

MALCOLM HAD JOINED THE DEBATE TEAM AT CHARLESTOWN. NOW, AT NORFOLK, HE JOINED AGAIN.

HIS BLEND OF CONTROLLED PASSION AND HUMOROUS CUNNING MADE HIM A NATURAL DEBATER AND EVANGELIST.

MALCOLM SPENT MUCH TIME DISCUSSING ELIJAH MUHAMMAD'S TEACHINGS WITH HIS FELLOW INMATES, ADOPTING REGINALD'S METHODS TO ENLIST NEW RECRUITS.

HE WOULD REVEAL THE TRUTH SLOWLY, ALLOWING IT TO SINK IN. THEN HE'D PAINT A PICTURE OF THE BLACK MAN'S GLORIOUS LIFE IN AFRICA, AND HIS ENSLAVEMENT BY THE WHITE MAN.

WHEN HE'D FINISH WITH THE REVELATION THAT THE WHITE MAN IS THE DEVIL, IT WAS, ACCORDING TO MALCOLM, "A PERFECT ECHO OF THAT BLACK CONVICT'S LIFELONG EXPERIENCE."

IT WORKED AS WELL ON OTHERS AS IT HAD ON HIM—AND HE HAD REGINALD TO THANK.

BUT WHEN REGINALD NEXT VISITED, IN THE FALL OF 1949, HE SEEMED AGITATED.

I HAVE BAD NEWS.

REGINALD WAS BEING PUNISHED FOR BREAKING NOI RULES— BUT HE BELIEVED ELIJAH MUHAMMAD WAS GUILTY OF THE SAME OFFENSES. DECLARING THE MESSENGER A FALSE PROPHET, REGINALD LEFT.

A SHORT TIME LATER, MALCOLM WAS TOLD THAT REGINALD HAD BEEN SUSPENDED FROM THE NOI BY ELIJAH MUHAMMAD FOR NOT PRACTICING "MORAL RESTRAINT."

EVEN AFTER HIS SUSPENSION, HOWEVER, REGINALD CONTINUED HIS AFFAIR WITH THE SECRETARY OF THE NOI'S NEW YORK TEMPLE.

MALCOLM WROTE ELIJAH MUHAMMAD, BEGGING LENIENCY FOR HIS BROTHER, BUT MUHAMMAD STOOD FIRM: REGINALD WAS OUT OF THE NOI.

HE IS PAYING FOR HIS SINS WITH THE CHASTISEMENT OF ALLAH.

LIKE HIS MOTHER BEFORE HIM, REGINALD'S MIND BEGAN TO FRAY UNDER THE PRESSURE. ELIJAH MUHAMMAD HAD LITTLE SYMPATHY.

MALCOLM CHOSE TO HONOR HIS VOW OF LIFELONG COMMITMENT TO ELIJAH MUHAMMAD...

...AND TURNED HIS BACK ON HIS BLOOD KIN.

MUCH LATER, MALCOLM WOULD DEEPLY REGRET HIS DECISION, BUT NOW HIS CHOICE WAS CLEAR.

THOUGH HE HAD LOST A BROTHER, MALCOLM'S RELATIONSHIP WITH ELIJAH MUHAMMAD GREW STRONGER THAN EVER. THE TWO REGULARLY COMMUNICATED BY MAIL, WITH MUHAMMAD SENDING MALCOLM BOOKS AND INFORMATION ON ISLAM AND THE NOI. . .

....AND ENCOURAGING MALCOLM TO CONTINUE HIS WORK CONVERTING HIS FELLOW PRISONERS TO ISLAM.

WHEN SPENDING ALL HIS TIME IN THE PRISON LIBRARY, MALCOLM HAD BEEN CONSIDERED A MODEL PRISONER. BUT AS HE EMBRACED HIS ROLE AS NOI ACTIVIST, HIS BEHAVIOR BECAME MORE PROBLEMATIC.

IN 1950, MALCOLM WAS TRANSFERRED BACK TO CHARLESTOWN, WHERE HIS DEMAND FOR A CELL FACING MECCA MADE THE BOSTON PAPERS.

52

CHAPTER EIGHT: *FREE AT LAST*

IN THE SUMMER OF 1952 THE PAROLE BOARD RELEASED MALCOLM, WHO PLEDGED TO JOIN HIS BROTHER WILFRED IN DETROIT.

WILFRED GOT MALCOLM A JOB IN THE FURNITURE STORE WHERE HE WAS MANAGER. MALCOLM WAS A MODEL EMPLOYEE.

MALCOLM AND WILFRED REGULARLY ATTENDED SERVICES AT THE NOI DETROIT TEMPLE NO. 1. BUT MALCOLM WAS BOTHERED BY THE NUMBER OF EMPTY SEATS. WILFRED SAID THAT ALLAH, IN TIME, WOULD FILL THEM.

BUT MALCOLM, BELIEVING THAT ALLAH HELPS THOSE WHO HELP THEMSELVES, HAD OTHER PLANS.

ON LABOR DAY 1952, MALCOLM JOINED A CARAVAN OF DETROIT TEMPLE MEMBERS ON A TRIP TO THE CHICAGO TEMPLE TO HEAR ELIJAH MUHAMMAD SPEAK.

SEEING THE MESSENGER WAS ONE OF THE HIGH POINTS OF MALCOLM'S LIFE, BUT WHAT HAPPENED AT THE CONCLUSION OF MUHAMMAD'S SERMON TOOK MALCOLM COMPLETELY BY SURPRISE.

ELIJAH MUHAMMAD HIMSELF CALLED OUT MALCOLM'S NAME, ASKING HIM TO RISE. WITH THE EYES OF THE CROWD UPON HIM, MUHAMMAD DESCRIBED MALCOLM'S YEARS OF INCARCERATION.

EVERY DAY, FOR YEARS, BROTHER MALCOLM HAS WRITTEN A LETTER FROM PRISON TO ME. AND I HAVE WRITTEN HIM AS OFTEN AS I COULD.

WE WILL SEE HOW HE DOES NOW. I BELIEVE THAT HE IS GOING TO REMAIN FAITHFUL.

FOR MALCOLM, IT WAS A VOTE OF CONFIDENCE FROM THE HIGHEST POSSIBLE SOURCE.

AFTERWARD, MUHAMMAD INVITED MALCOLM TO HIS HOME FOR DINNER. DURING A QUIET MOMENT, MALCOLM RAISED A QUESTION THAT HAD BEEN ON HIS MIND.

MR. MUHAMMAD, HOW MANY MUSLIMS ARE SUPPOSED TO BE IN OUR TEMPLE NO. 1 IN DETROIT?

THERE ARE SUPPOSED TO BE THOUSANDS.

SIR, WHAT IS YOUR OPINION OF THE BEST WAY OF GETTING THOUSANDS THERE?

GO AFTER THE YOUNG PEOPLE. ONCE YOU GET THEM, THE OLDER ONES WILL FOLLOW THROUGH SHAME!

MALCOLM HAD HIS MARCHING ORDERS. FIRED WITH ENTHUSIASM, HE STARTED A DRIVE FOR CONVERTS, AN EFFORT THAT THE NOI MEMBERSHIP CALLED "FISHING."

BUT MALCOLM HAD MORE THAN ENTHUSIASM WORKING FOR HIM. HE WAS GOOD-LOOKING, INTELLIGENT, AND KNEW WHAT WAS ON THE MINDS OF YOUNG BLACK PEOPLE IN THE CITY.

HEAR HOW THE WHITE MAN KIDNAPPED AND ROBBED AND RAPED OUR BLACK RACE!

OF
I AM

EVERY CITY MALCOLM VISITED REPORTED SHARP INCREASES IN MEMBERSHIP.

THAT SEPTEMBER, MALCOLM WAS GIVEN AN X TO REPLACE HIS "SLAVE NAME" OF LITTLE. ACCORDING TO ELIJAH MUHAMMAD, THE SLAVE NAME HAD BEEN FORCED UPON HIS ANCESTORS BY SLAVE OWNERS; THE BLACK MAN'S TRUE HISTORICAL NAME WOULD REMAIN LOST "UNTIL ALLAH GIVES US A HOLY NAME FROM HIS OWN MOUTH."

AT EVERY OPPORTUNITY, AND FOR EVERY POSSIBLE ACHIEVE-MENT, MALCOLM GAVE ELIJAH MUHAMMAD THE CREDIT.

THE TWO WERE INSEPARABLE; MUHAMMAD OFTEN HINTED THAT MALCOLM WOULD LEAD THE NOI ONCE HE WAS GONE.

BUT EVEN AS MALCOLM WORKED TO GROW THE NOI, RACE RELATIONS IN AMERICA WERE BEING RESHAPED IN OTHER WAYS.

IN 1954, IN THE CASE OF BROWN VS. BOARD OF EDUCATION, THE SUPREME COURT OVERTURNED THE CYNICAL DOCTRINE OF "SEPARATE BUT EQUAL."

THE DOCTRINE, WHICH HAD BEEN THE LAW OF THE LAND SINCE 1896, WAS ARGUED AGAINST BY A BLACK LAWYER NAMED THURGOOD MARSHALL, WHO, IN 1967, WOULD BECOME THE FIRST BLACK SUPREME COURT JUSTICE.

HIGH COURT BANS SEGREG
IN PUBLIC SCHOOLS
Budge Wins 3 Titles,

MARSHALL CONVINCED THE COURT TO REJECT "SEPARATE BUT EQUAL" TREATMENT FOR BLACKS. "DOES SEGREGATION OF CHILDREN IN PUBLIC SCHOOLS SOLELY ON THE BASIS OF RACE," JUSTICE EARL WARREN ASKED, "DEPRIVE THE CHILDREN OF THE MINORITY GROUP OF EQUAL EDUCATIONAL OPPORTUNITIES? WE BELIEVE THAT IT DOES."

ON DECEMBER 1, 1955, IN MONTGOMERY, ALABAMA, ROSA PARKS REFUSED TO GIVE UP HER SEAT ON THE BUS TO A WHITE PASSENGER AND WAS JAILED.

THE NATIONAL ASSOCIATION FOR THE ADVANCEMENT OF COLORED PEOPLE WAS ALERTED TO HER SITUATION AND BY MONDAY, THE SEGREGATED BUS SYSTEM WAS BEING BOYCOTTED.

I AM A MAN

END UN-EQUAL RIGHTS

NOW!

WE MARCH FOR INTEGRATED SCHOOLS

JOBS

LEADING THE BOYCOTT WAS A YOUNG MINISTER NAMED MARTIN LUTHER KING JR., WHOSE POLITIC MANNER AND RICH SPEAKING VOICE ATTRACTED INSTANT ATTENTION.

ALTHOUGH THE SUPREME COURT DECLARED MONTGOMERY'S SEGREGATED TRANSIT SYSTEM UNCONSTITUTIONAL, ROSA PARKS LEFT MONTGOMERY FOR DETROIT IN 1957 TO ESCAPE DEATH THREATS.

IN 1957, THE NAACP ARRANGED FOR NINE TOP AFRICAN-AMERICAN STUDENTS TO ENROLL IN LITTLE ROCK, ARKANSAS' ALL-WHITE CENTRAL HIGH SCHOOL.

ON SEPTEMBER 2, ARKANSAS GOVERNOR ORVAL FAUBUS CALLED IN THE NATIONAL GUARD TO KEEP THE STUDENTS OUT OF THE BUILDING.

WHEN THEY TRIED AGAIN, ARMED THIS TIME WITH A COURT ORDER, THEY WERE MET BY AN ANGRY MOB.

LITTLE ROCK'S MAYOR REQUESTED FEDERAL TROOPS TO COMPLY WITH THE COURT ORDER, AND PRESIDENT EISENHOWER AGREED.

THE FOLLOWING YEAR, GOVERNOR FAUBUS CLOSED THE SCHOOL.

TO ADDRESS CIVIL RIGHTS ISSUES THROUGHOUT THE SOUTH, MARTIN LUTHER KING ORGANIZED THE SOUTHERN CHRISTIAN LEADERSHIP CONFERENCE (SCLC), WHICH FOLLOWED KING'S INTERPRETATION OF CHRISTIAN PRINCIPLES ON NONVIOLENCE—AND INDIAN LEADER MAHATMA GANDHI'S PRACTICES.

MAN MUST EVOLVE FOR ALL HUMAN CONFLICT A METHOD THAT REJECTS REVENGE, AGGRESSION, AND RETALIATION. THE FOUNDATION OF SUCH A METHOD IS LOVE.

KING NOW HAD THE EAR OF WHITE AMERICA, WHETHER IT WANTED TO LISTEN OR NOT. MALCOLM, THE DARK REFLECTION OF KING'S HOPEFUL MESSAGE, HAD NOT YET FOUND A WAY TO REACH THAT AUDIENCE.

FOR ALL OF MALCOLM'S SUCCESS INCREASING NOI MEMBERSHIP, FEW OUTSIDE THE URBAN BLACK COMMUNITIES KNEW OF THE NATION. MALCOLM'S LONG-STANDING AMBITION TO TELL OFF THE WHITE MAN TO HIS FACE REMAINED UNREALIZED.

BUT THE NOI HAD ATTRACTED THE ATTENTION OF THE FBI, WHO HAD BEEN KEEPING AN EYE ON MALCOLM SINCE HE'D CLAIMED IN A LETTER FROM PRISON TO HAVE "ALWAYS BEEN A COMMUNIST."

MALCOLM KNEW THEY WERE BEING WATCHED. FBI AGENTS HAD INTERVIEWED THE COWORKERS AND BOSSES OF NOI MEMBERS, OFTEN ENDANGERING THEIR JOBS.

YOU KNOW THEM ISLAM NEGROES ARE COMMIES, RIGHT?

AS THE NOI GREW, SO DID THE FBI'S INTEREST. WHILE WHITE AMERICA REMAINED LARGELY IGNORANT OF THE NOI'S PROGRESS, THE BUREAU WATCHED EVERY STEP.

FBI DIRECTOR J. EDGAR HOOVER BEGAN WIRETAPPING NOI PHONE LINES. ADAMANTLY RACIST, HE CLAIMED THE TAPS WERE NECESSARY DUE TO THE NOI'S "VIOLENT NATURE," DESPITE THE FACT THAT NOI MEMBERS WERE FORBIDDEN TO CARRY WEAPONS OF ANY KIND.

THE FBI DID LITTLE TO HIDE THEIR INTEREST IN THE NOI. WHEN WORD OF THEIR ONGOING INVESTIGATION SURFACED, THE NEW YORK POLICE DEPARTMENT OF SPECIAL SERVICES RESPONDED BY ASSIGNING UNDER-COVER AGENTS TO SHADOW ITS MEMBERS AND NEW MOSQUE NO. 7 LEADER, MALCOLM X.

CHAPTER NINE: *A NEW LEADER*

AN ACT OF VIOLENCE COMMITTED IN APRIL 1957, HOWEVER, DID BRING MALCOLM AND THE NATION OF ISLAM INTO THE NATIONAL SPOTLIGHT.

ONE VERSION OF THE STORY HAS IT THAT TWO WHITE POLICEMEN IN HARLEM SAVAGELY BEAT A DRUNK MAN.

ONE OBSERVER, AN NOI BROTHER NAMED JOHNSON X HINTON, WAS INCENSED.

JERKS. YOU'RE NOT IN ALABAMA—

DISGUSTED, HINTON TURNED TO LEAVE, UNAWARE THAT HE HAD SUCCEEDED IN REDIRECTING THE POLICEMEN'S RAGE.

NUGGGHHH!!

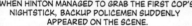

WHEN HINTON MANAGED TO GRAB THE FIRST COP'S NIGHTSTICK, BACKUP POLICEMEN SUDDENLY APPEARED ON THE SCENE.

OTHERS SAY THAT HINTON WAS IN A HARLEM PRECINCT JAIL CELL PRAYING WHEN THE NIGHTSTICKS CAME DOWN.

IN EITHER EVENT, WORD OF THE BRUTALITY QUICKLY SPREAD ACROSS HARLEM.

FURIOUS, RESIDENTS FLOCKED TO THE PRECINCT HOUSE TO DEMAND JUSTICE.

IN A PANIC, SOME SAY, THE POLICE PHONED MALCOLM ASKING FOR HELP.

NOW IT WAS THE POLICE WHO WERE OUTNUMBERED.

HOWEVER HE GOT THE NEWS, MALCOLM MOBILIZED THE NOI IMMEDIATELY AND WAS ON HIS WAY.

THE PARAMILITARY UNIT OF THE NOI KNOWN AS THE FRUIT OF ISLAM (FOI) ARRIVED, POSITIONING THEMSELVES TO MAINTAIN ORDER.

"IT WAS ALL I COULD DO TO CONTAIN MYSELF," MALCOLM REMEMBERED. "HE WAS SEMICONSCIOUS. BLOOD BATHED HIS HEAD, FACE, AND SHOULDERS."

MALCOLM DEMANDED THAT BROTHER JOHNSON RECEIVE IMMEDIATE MEDICAL ATTENTION.

THE AMBULANCE ARRIVED, AND A CROWD OF MORE THAN 2,000 FOLLOWED IT TO THE HOSPITAL ON FOOT.

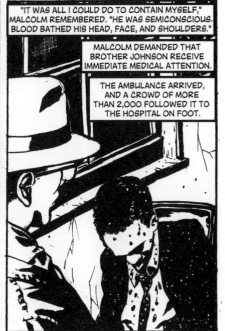

WHEN MALCOLM ARRIVED, HE WAS SHOCKED BY HINTON'S INJURIES.

WHEN MALCOLM WAS SATISFIED THAT HINTON WOULD BE TAKEN CARE OF, HE STEPPED OUT OF THE HOSPITAL AND WAVED HIS HAND...

...AND THE FRUIT OF ISLAM PEACEFULLY DISPERSED THE CROWD.

POLICE INSPECTOR MAGOWAN OBSERVED MALCOLM'S POWERFUL ACT OF CROWD CONTROL WITH A MIXTURE OF IN AWE AND APPREHENSION.

NO MAN SHOULD HAVE THAT KIND OF POWER...

AMSTERDAM NEWS EDITOR JAMES HICKS ADDED:

WHAT HE *REALLY* MEANT IS THAT NO *BLACK* MAN SHOULD HAVE THAT KIND OF POWER.

WHATEVER THE EXACT EVENTS OF THAT DAY, WHAT IS CERTAIN IS THAT NOT ONLY HAD MALCOLM BECOME A HERO TO THE BLACK PEOPLE OF HARLEM...

...BUT HE AND THE NATION OF ISLAM HAD MADE THEIR FIRST STEP INTO THE CONSCIOUSNESS OF WHITE AMERICA.

MALCOLM'S INTENSE SCHEDULE LEFT HIM LITTLE PERSONAL TIME—BUT AS HIS PUBLIC STATURE SHOT UP, MALCOLM SEEMED DRIVEN TO PUT DOWN ROOTS AS WELL.

IN DECEMBER OF 1957, HE SOUGHT MUHAMMAD'S BLESSING TO MARRY COLLEGE-EDUCATED NOI SISTER BETTY X, FORMERLY BETTY SAUNDERS.

THE MESSENGER'S VERDICT: SISTER BETTY X WAS A FINE SISTER.

WITH MUHAMMAD'S BLESSING IN HAND, MALCOLM DROVE TO LANSING.

JUST OUTSIDE DETROIT, HE STOPPED AT A GAS STATION AND CALLED BETTY.

OH HELLO, BROTHER MINISTER.

LOOK, DO YOU WANT TO GET MARRIED?

THE MOST CALCULATING OF SPEAKERS, HE LATER CLAIMED HE DIDN'T KNOW WHAT HE WAS GOING TO SAY TO HER UNTIL HE SAID IT.

YES.

"JUST LIKE I KNEW SHE WOULD," MALCOLM ADMITTED.

WELL, I DON'T HAVE A WHOLE LOT OF TIME, YOU'D BETTER CATCH A PLANE TO DETROIT.

THEY WERE MARRIED IN LANSING TWO DAYS LATER, ON JANUARY 14, 1958. BY NOVEMBER, THE FIRST OF THEIR SIX DAUGHTERS WAS BORN.

IN JULY 1959, THE FIRST PART OF A FIVE-PART DOCUMENTARY SERIES HOSTED BY MIKE WALLACE WAS BROADCAST.

THE HATE THAT HATE PRODUCED

IT PURPORTED TO REVEAL THE TRUE HISTORY AND CURRENT STATE OF THE NOI.

ALTHOUGH THE SERIES WAS PRODUCED WITH THE FULL PARTICIPATION OF MALCOLM, MUHAMMAD, AND MANY MEMBERS OF THE NOI...

...AND NOTHING ANY NOI MEMBER SAID OR DID WAS PARTICULARLY THREATENING...

...THE DOCUMENTARY WAS EDITED IN SUCH A WAY THAT THE JUXTAPOSED IMAGES WERE OMINOUS.

AND IF THE IMAGES ALONE DIDN'T SCARE THE DAYLIGHTS OUT OF WHITE AMERICA...

...MIKE WALLACE'S NARRATION WOULD DO THE TRICK.

WHILE CITY OFFICIALS, STATE AGENCIES, WHITE LIBERALS, AND SOBER-MINDED NEGROES STAND IDLY BY, A GROUP OF NEGRO DISSENTERS ARE TAKING TO STREET-CORNER STEPLADDERS...

...CHURCH PULPITS, SPORTS ARENAS, AND BALLROOM PLATFORMS ACROSS THE NATION TO PREACH A GOSPEL OF HATE THAT WOULD SET OFF A FEDERAL INVESTIGATION IF IT WERE TO BE PREACHED BY SOUTHERN WHITES.

VIEWERS WERE LEFT WITH THE IMPRESSION THAT THE NOI WAS A CLEAR AND PRESENT THREAT TO AMERICA.

MALCOLM WAS MORE THAN HAPPY TO CONCUR. NEW RECRUITS POURED INTO THE NOI.

AFTER *THE HATE THAT HATE PRODUCED* APPEARED, THE NOI RECEIVED TWO TYPES OF CALLS.

THE FIRST WAS FOR INTERVIEWS WITH THE SHOCKING "ANGRY NEGROES." *LOOK, NEWSWEEK,* AND *TIME* DID FEATURE-LENGTH STORIES ABOUT LIFE IN THE NATION OF ISLAM.

WRITER/DIRECTOR/PHOTOGRAPHER GORDON PARKS'S PHOTO ESSAY ON "THE BLACK MUSLIMS" FOR *LIFE* MAGAZINE WAS AMONG THE MOST INFLUENTIAL.

WHILE WRITING A *READER'S DIGEST* PIECE, "MR. MUHAMMAD SPEAKS," ALEX HALEY MET MALCOLM X.

THEIR RELATIONSHIP WOULD GO FROM A CLASSIC *PLAYBOY* INTERVIEW TO *THE AUTOBIOGRAPHY OF MALCOLM X,* ONE OF THE BEST-SELLING AUTOBIOGRAPHIES OF ALL TIME.

THE SECOND TYPE OF CALL WAS THE ONE MADE TO EXPRESS HATE. *THE HATE THAT HATE PRODUCED* ANGERED MANY PEOPLE ACROSS THE COUNTRY WHO HAD SEEN IT...

...AND THEY FELT COMPELLED TO SHARE THE HATE THE PROGRAM PRODUCED.

IN THE SOUTH, A NEW FORM OF PROTEST—SIT-INS AT SEGREGATED LUNCHROOM COUNTERS—CAUGHT THE EYE OF THE SCLC. BUT SOME FELT IT MOVED TOO SLOWLY AND WAS NOT IN TOUCH WITH THE YOUNGER GENERATION OF BLACKS.

THESE CONCERNS LED TO THE CREATION OF THE STUDENT NONVIOLENT COORDINATING COMMITTEE (SNCC).

THE CONGRESS OF RACIAL EQUALITY (CORE), FOUNDED IN THE 1940S, ALSO EMBRACED GANDHI'S NONVIOLENT TACTICS.

TO DESEGREGATE THE SOUTH'S BUS LINES, CORE, WORKING WITH THE SNCC, FILLED BUSES WITH "FREEDOM RIDERS."

THE RIDERS WERE HARASSED AND BEATEN, ULTIMATELY REQUIRING THE ASSISTANCE OF THE FEDERAL GOVERNMENT.

ALTHOUGH BLACKS OUTNUMBERED WHITES IN MANY SOUTHERN DISTRICTS, FEW WERE REGISTERED TO VOTE.

IN MISSISSIPPI, ALABAMA, AND GEORGIA, CORE AND THE SNCC BEGAN MASSIVE VOTER REGISTRATION DRIVES.

BUT REGISTERING COULD BE DANGEROUS. MIDDLE-AGED FANNIE LOU HAMER WAS ONE OF MANY BLACKS BEATEN AND THROWN IN JAIL AFTER REGISTERING TO VOTE WITH THE SNCC'S SUPPORT.

IN JUNE 1963, NAACP MEMBER MEDGAR EVERS WAS SHOT IN HIS JACKSON, MISSISSIPPI, DRIVEWAY AS HE WALKED TO HIS HOME WITH AN ARMFUL OF "JIM CROW MUST GO" T-SHIRTS.

AND IN SEPTEMBER FOUR BLACK GIRLS WERE KILLED WHEN THE KU KLUX KLAN BOMBED THEIR CHURCH IN BIRMINGHAM, ALABAMA.

MALCOLM'S CONFRONTATIONAL APPROACH WAS NOW BEGINNING TO MAKE MORE SENSE TO YOUNG BLACKS THAN DR. KING'S POLICIES OF NONVIOLENCE.

IN THE SUMMER OF 1963, WHILE MILLIONS OF BLACKS JOINED KING FOR HIS MARCH ON WASHINGTON, MALCOLM WATCHED, EVEN THOUGH ELIJAH MUHAMMAD HAD FORBIDDEN IT.

MALCOLM, WHO WAS SERVING AS INTERIM MINISTER AT THE WASHINGTON, DC, MOSQUE AT THE TIME, LATER SARCASTICALLY NOTED THAT "WHILE KING WAS HAVING A DREAM, THE REST OF US NEGROES ARE HAVING A NIGHTMARE."

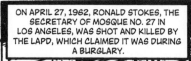

ON APRIL 27, 1962, RONALD STOKES, THE SECRETARY OF MOSQUE NO. 27 IN LOS ANGELES, WAS SHOT AND KILLED BY THE LAPD, WHICH CLAIMED IT WAS DURING A BURGLARY.

BUT MALCOLM SAID THAT STOKES, HIS WIFE, AND A FRIEND WERE RETURNING TO THE MOSQUE WITH LAUNDRY FROM A DRY CLEANER WHEN THEY WERE STOPPED BY TWO LAPD OFFICERS.

YOU GOT A LICENSE TO SELL CLOTHING?

LOOK, OFFICER— I'M NOT SELLING THESE CLOTHES, AND THEY WEREN'T STOLEN.

NO? I HEAR YOU GUYS ARE ALWAYS STEALING THINGS.

EXCUSE ME?

YEAH... STEALING FROM WHITE FOLKS.

WE HAVEN'T DONE ANYTHING.

THAT'S ALLOWED, RIGHT? STEALIN'? AS LONG AS THEY'RE WHITE.

AS HIS WIFE RACED BACK TO THE MOSQUE, STOKES TRIED TO HANDLE THE LAPD, BUT THE COP WAS LOOKING FOR TROUBLE.

LOOK, I KNOW YOU'RE ONLY DOING THIS BECAUSE WE'RE MUSLIMS...

...BUT IF YOU JUST CALM DOWN WE CAN—

STOP TALKING WITH YOUR HANDS! YOU PEOPLE'RE ALWAYS TALKING WITH YOUR HANDS!

SEE? MUCH BETTER!

ARRRRRR!!

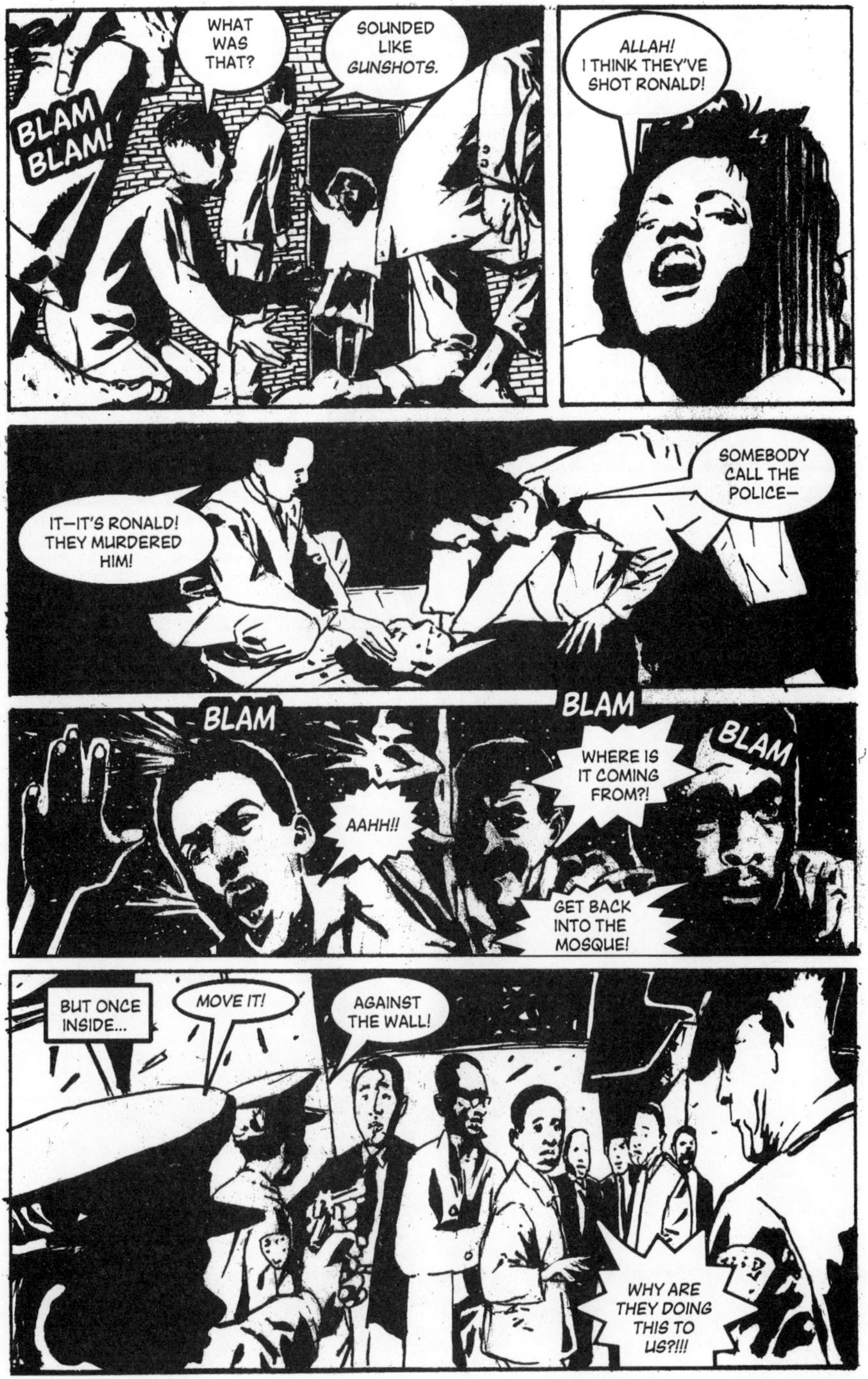
BLAM
BLAM!
WHAT WAS THAT?
SOUNDED LIKE GUNSHOTS.
ALLAH! I THINK THEY'VE SHOT RONALD!
IT—IT'S RONALD! THEY MURDERED HIM!
SOMEBODY CALL THE POLICE—
BLAM
AAHH!!
BLAM
WHERE IS IT COMING FROM?!
BLAM
GET BACK INTO THE MOSQUE!
BUT ONCE INSIDE...
MOVE IT!
AGAINST THE WALL!
WHY ARE THEY DOING THIS TO US?!!!

RONALD STOKES DIED IN A POOL OF HIS OWN BLOOD FROM A GUNSHOT TO THE HEAD. THE INJURED MUSLIMS WERE HELD FOR BAIL AND HAD TO WAIT DAYS TO RECEIVE TREATMENT FOR THEIR WOUNDS.

THE ATTACK SEEMED TO HAVE THE APPROVAL OF WILLIAM H. PARKER, THE LAPD CHIEF, WHO STOOD BEHIND THE TALE HIS MEN HAD TOLD OF A BURGLARY GONE BAD.

MUHAMMAD SENT MALCOLM TO LOS ANGELES TO MINISTER AT THE VICTIM'S FUNERAL. MALCOLM HAD BEEN A CLOSE FRIEND OF STOKES; HIS MURDER HAD HIT HIM HARD. BUT HE WAS ALREADY THINKING ABOUT THE SERMON HE'D DELIVER—THERE WAS MUCH TO BE SAID.

MALCOLM FELT THAT AS PUBLIC AWARENESS OF THE NOI GREW, SO WOULD ACTS OF VIOLENCE AGAINST THEM. WHEN ATTACKED, THE NOI SHOULD RESPOND IN A LIKE MANNER.

THE POSSIBILITY OF NOI REPRISALS ALONE WOULD MAKE POTENTIAL AGGRESSORS THINK TWICE BEFORE ASSAULTING MUSLIMS.

BUT MUHAMMAD FORBID MALCOLM TO EXPRESS THIS OPINION, INSISTING THAT FURTHER VIOLENCE MUST BE AVOIDED.

MALCOLM DEFERRED TO MUHAMMAD'S WISHES, BUT REMAINED CONVINCED THAT THE NOI WOULD NEED TO CHANGE TO SURVIVE.

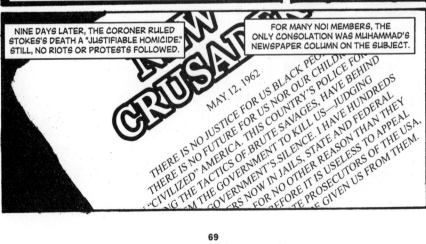

NINE DAYS LATER, THE CORONER RULED STOKES'S DEATH A "JUSTIFIABLE HOMICIDE." STILL, NO RIOTS OR PROTESTS FOLLOWED.

FOR MANY NOI MEMBERS, THE ONLY CONSOLATION WAS MUHAMMAD'S NEWSPAPER COLUMN ON THE SUBJECT.

NEW CRUSAD

MAY 12, 1962

THERE IS NO JUSTICE FOR US BLACK PEO... THERE IS NO FUTURE FOR US NOR OUR CHILDR... "CIVILIZED" AMERICA. THIS COUNTRY'S POLICE FOR... ...G THE TACTICS OF BRUTE SAVAGES, HAVE BEHIND ...M THE GOVERNMENT TO KILL US...JUDGING ...GOVERNMENT'S SILENCE. I HAVE HUNDRED... ...RS NOW IN JAILS, STATE AND FEDERAL ...FOR NO OTHER REASON THAN THEY ...BEFORE IT IS USELESS TO APPEAL ...TE PROSECUTORS OF THE USA, ...E GIVEN US FROM THEM.

CHAPTER TEN: SINS OF THE FATHER

MALCOLM COMPLAINED TO HIS HARLEM MOSQUE ASSOCIATES ABOUT THE ARTICLE. SIMPLY POINTING OUT INJUSTICE, HE FELT, AMOUNTED TO BACKING DOWN.

ALL TALK, AND NO ACTION.

THE OTHER MINISTERS, JEALOUS OF MALCOLM, REPORTED HIS SENTIMENTS BACK TO AN INCREASINGLY EXASPERATED MUHAMMAD.

I DON'T KNOW WHO'S GOING TO CONTROL MALCOLM— JUST TELL HIM TO COOL HIS HEELS.

INSTEAD OF CONSIDERING MALCOLM'S SELF DEFENSE PROPOSALS, MUHAMMAD CHOSE INSTEAD TO CONCENTRATE ON WAYS TO SILENCE MALCOLM.

ELIJAH MUHAMMAD WAS UNDER SERIOUS PRESSURE. HIS HEALTH WAS FAILING AND HIS TOP MINISTER WAS BECOMING A LIABILITY. THEN HE RECEIVED A PHONE CALL THAT THREATENED TO EXPOSE HIS GREATEST SECRET...

YOU'LL SEE, ELIJAH! I'LL LEAVE YOU FOR SOMEONE ELSE—

THE WOMAN WAS MUHAMMAD'S FORMER PERSONAL SECRETARY— ONE OF SEVEN HE'D HAD EXTRAMARITAL RELATIONS WITH.

HOW CAN YOU SAY SUCH THINGS? COME ON, DON'T TALK LIKE THAT...

NONE OF THE SEVEN WOMEN— SIX OF WHOM HAD GIVEN BIRTH TO THE MESSENGER'S CHILDREN— KNEW ABOUT THE OTHERS... UNTIL NOW.

BUT IF YOU TRY A TRICK LIKE THAT AGAIN—

CLIK-K-K-CK—

THE FBI WIRETAPS RECORDED IT ALL.

IN HIS AUTOBIOGRAPHY, MALCOLM SAYS HINTS OF MUHAMMAD'S INDISCRETIONS DATED BACK AS FAR AS 1955. BUT HIS BROTHER REGINALD HAD INSISTED IN 1949, WHEN HE WAS "ISOLATED" FOR HIS OWN SEXUAL INDISCRETION, THAT MUHAMMAD WAS GUILTY EVEN THEN.

THE IDEA THAT THE MESSENGER HIMSELF MIGHT ACT IMMORALLY WAS SO UNBELIEVABLE TO MALCOLM THAT HE HAD DISOWNED HIS BROTHER, WHO EVENTUALLY WENT MAD.

BUT IF MUHAMMAD HAD ACTED IMMORALLY, CONDEMNING REGINALD FOR SIMILAR ACTS WAS THE HEIGHT OF HYPOCRISY.

MALCOLM NEEDED TO KNOW IF THE RUMORS WERE TRUE.

IN CHICAGO TO ATTEND THE ANNUAL "SAVIOUR'S DAY" CONVENTION, MALCOLM INTENDED TO CONFRONT THE ONE MAN WHO COULD TELL HIM. BUT MUHAMMAD DECIDED NOT TO APPEAR.

MALCOLM INSTEAD APPROACHED THE PROPHET'S SON WALLACE, ONE OF THE NOI'S MOST RESPECTED MINISTERS...

...WHO CONFIRMED HIS WORST FEARS.

ALL THE MESSENGER'S SECRETARIES WERE YOUNG, SINGLE, AND NAIVE. THE AFFAIRS HAD CONTINUED FOR YEARS.

BUT THE TRUTH COULD NO LONGER BE HIDDEN. TWO OF THE WOMEN WERE FILING PATERNITY SUITS.

WALLACE SAID THAT ONCE IT WAS OBVIOUS THAT THE SECRETARIES WERE PREGNANT, MUHAMMAD WOULD SUSPEND THEM FROM THE NOI FOR BREAKING THE RULES AGAINST ADULTERY AND FORNICATION.

THE IRONY BORDERED ON THE SADISTIC... OR THE INSANE.

WANTING TO SPEAK TO THE WOMEN, MALCOLM ASKED FOR A LIST OF THEIR NAMES. AS WALLACE RATTLED THEM OFF, MALCOLM WAS STUNNED SPEECHLESS.

HE KNEW ALL THE WOMEN— IF FACT, HE'D HIRED THEM FOR THE JOBS, AND HAD CASUALLY DATED TWO OF THEM. EVEN MORE MONSTROUS: HE REMEMBERED THAT MUHAMMAD HAD CONSIDERED BETTY X FOR ONE OF THE POSITIONS JUST BEFORE SHE AND MALCOLM HAD ELOPED.

MALCOLM WAS SICK WITH SHAME. HE HAD BEEN TRICKED INTO ONCE AGAIN EXPLOITING YOUNG, INNOCENT BLACK WOMEN FOR IMMORAL PURPOSES.

COULD THE NOI POSSIBLY WEATHER A SCANDAL OF THIS MAGNITUDE? MALCOLM WAS DETERMINED TO SEE THAT IT DID.

HE WOULD START BY CONTACTING THE SECRETARIES TO GET THEIR SIDE OF THE STORY.

BY CONTACTING THE WOMEN, MALCOLM WAS BREAKING THE RULE THAT FORBID NOI MEMBERS FROM SPEAKING TO "ISOLATED" MUSLIMS. BUT IT WAS A RULE HE NOW DEEPLY REGRETTED HAVING OBEYED IN THE PAST.

THE WOMEN CONFIRMED ALL THE RUMORS, AND ADDED SOMETHING MORE: MUHAMMAD HAD SPOKEN TO THEM OF MALCOLM.

HE IS MY GREATEST MINISTER, BUT SOMEDAY HE WILL LEAVE, TURN AGAINST ME—SO HE IS DANGEROUS.

NO LONGER ABLE TO DENY MUHAMMAD'S TRANSGRESSIONS, MALCOLM, WORKING WITH WALLACE, SEARCHED BIBLICAL AND ISLAMIC TEXTS TO RATIONALIZE THE ACTS OF THEIR MESSENGER.

THEY SOUGHT EXAMPLES THAT TAUGHT "A MAN'S ACCOMPLISHMENTS IN HIS LIFE OUTWEIGH HIS PERSONAL, HUMAN WEAKNESSES."

LIKE DAVID, WHO REMAINS A HERO FOR SLAYING GOLIATH DESPITE COMMITTING ADULTERY WITH BATHSHEBA. ON BALANCE, DAVID WAS GOOD.

OR MOSES, WHOSE OWN ACT OF ADULTERY IS LOST TO TIME, WHILE HIS REPUTATION AS THE JEWS' EMANCIPATOR LIVES FOREVER. ON BALANCE, MOSES TOO WAS GOOD.

IF THESE LESSONS COULD BE TAUGHT AND ASSIMILATED BEFORE THE NEWS BROKE, MALCOLM BELIEVED THE FLOCK WOULD NOT REJECT THE MESSENGER. THE NOI WOULD BE SAVED.

BUT THE PLAN WAS AN ACT OF DESPERATION, A MASSIVE COMPROMISE OF ALL OF MALCOLM'S VALUES.

THE MINISTER WHO PREACHED THAT ALL OF HISTORY BOILED DOWN TO EITHER BLACK OR WHITE...

...WAS ABOUT TO COMMIT HIMSELF TO A WORLD OF GRAY.

MALCOLM WENT TO MUHAMMAD'S HOME IN ARIZONA EXPECTING A DIFFICULT MEETING. INSTEAD, IT SEEMED SURREAL.

WELL, SON— WHAT IS ON YOUR MIND?

WHEN MALCOLM ASKED IF THE RUMORS WERE TRUE, MUHAMMAD ADMITTED THEY WERE—WITHOUT EVEN A TRACE OF REGRET.

MALCOLM THEN SUGGESTED TEACHING THAT WHEN A GOOD MAN IS UNABLE TO STOP HIMSELF FROM DOING A BAD THING, THE PERFORMANCE OF THE BAD THING COULD BE TAUGHT TO MUSLIMS AS THE "FULFILLMENT OF PROPHESY."

MUHAMMAD SEEMED TO APPROVE.

SON, I'M NOT SURPRISED. YOU ALWAYS HAVE HAD SUCH A GOOD UNDERSTANDING OF PROPHESY AND OF SPIRITUAL THINGS. YOU RECOGNIZE THAT'S WHAT ALL OF THIS IS—PROPHESY.

YOU HAVE THE KIND OF UNDERSTANDING THAT ONLY AN OLD MAN HAS.

I'M DAVID. WHEN YOU READ ABOUT HOW DAVID TOOK ANOTHER MAN'S WIFE, I'M THAT DAVID.

YOU READ ABOUT NOAH, WHO GOT DRUNK—THAT'S ME.

YOU READ ABOUT LOT, WHO WENT AND LAID UP WITH HIS OWN DAUGHTERS.

I HAVE TO FULFILL ALL THOSE THINGS.

MALCOLM LEFT THE MEETING DAZED. HE HAD ASSUMED THAT MUHAMMAD WOULD BE GRATEFUL FOR ANY CREDIBLE EXCUSE TO EXTRICATE HIMSELF FROM THE PIT OF SIN HE WAS DROWNING IN.

INSTEAD HE FOUND A SEXUALLY OBSESSED OLD MAN WITH DELUSIONS OF GRANDEUR.

WALLACE MUHAMMAD, WHO HAD ALREADY TRIED TO SHAKE THE MADNESS OUT OF HIS FATHER, HAD BEEN SUSPENDED FROM THE NOI FOR HIS TROUBLES.

HE HAD COME TO BELIEVE THAT HIS FATHER, AFTER BEING TOLD HE WAS THE MESSENGER FOR SO MANY YEARS, ACCEPTED IT NOW AS UNSHAKABLE TRUTH.

UNTIL VERY RECENTLY, MALCOLM HAD, TOO.

BUT WHILE MUHAMMAD WAS INCREASINGLY LOST TO HIM, MALCOLM'S OBLIGATION TO THE NOI CONTINUED.

HE CONTACTED THE MINISTERS OF THE SIX LARGEST EAST COAST MOSQUES, TOLD THEM OF MUHAMMAD'S AFFAIRS, AND SUGGESTED THEY BEGIN TEACHING THE "FULFILLMENT OF PROPHESY" BEFORE THE SORDID STORY WENT PUBLIC.

SOME OF THE MINISTERS, INCLUDING LOUIS X (LATER LOUIS FARRAKHAN), ASSURED MALCOLM THEY'D ALREADY KNOWN ABOUT THE RUMORS FOR MONTHS...

...BUT THEY TOLD THE MESSENGER THAT MALCOLM WAS SPREADING FALSE RUMORS.

THE BREAKDOWN OF TRUST BETWEEN MALCOLM AND MUHAMMAD WAS ALMOST COMPLETE. THEIR NEXT CONFLICT WOULD DESTROY THEIR RELATIONSHIP FOREVER.

RECENT POLICE RAIDS OF MOSQUES IN LOUISIANA AND NEW YORK REMINDED MALCOLM OF THE NEED FOR THE NOI TO AGGRESSIVELY DEFEND ITSELF.

DESPITE MALCOLM'S GROWING CONCERN, MUHAMMAD REMAINED UNWILLING TO ABANDON HIS MODERATE POLICIES.

THEN, ON NOVEMBER 22, 1963:

BLAM!

THE MOST POWERFUL WHITE MAN IN THE WORLD HAD BEEN BROUGHT DOWN BY AN ACT OF VIOLENCE. THE NATION CAUGHT ITS COLLECTIVE BREATH, AND THEN CONSIDERED HOW BEST TO MOURN.

TELEVI
PPLIAN

JOURNALISTS AND PHOTOGRAPHERS CANVASSED THE COUNTRY, GATHERING DRAMATIC WORDS AND IMAGES FROM A COUNTRY IN PAIN.

ELIJAH MUHAMMAD OFFERED A MORE JARRING REACTION...

THIS ISN'T A DAY OF MOURNING FOR THE MUSLIMS. THAT DEVIL'S DEATH DOESN'T CONCERN US.

IT'S TIME FOR THE CHRISTIANS TO MOURN, NOT THE MUSLIMS.

MUHAMMAD SOON RECONSIDERED, AND RAN KENNEDY'S PORTRAIT ON THE COVER OF THE NOI NEWSPAPER MUHAMMAD SPEAKS.

BUT FBI WIRETAPS PICKED UP MUHAMMAD'S TRUE SENTIMENTS...

AFTER ALL, HE WASN'T THAT BAD...FOR A DEVIL.

MUHAMMAD COULD MAKE COMMENTS OF QUESTIONABLE TASTE BECAUSE HE KNEW, MUCH TO HIS CHAGRIN, THAT OUTSIDE THE NOI FEW LISTENED TO WHAT HE HAD TO SAY.

BUT MALCOLM COMMANDED THE ATTENTION OF A HUGE CROSS-SECTION OF THE PUBLIC...

...WHICH MADE MUHAMMAD INCREASINGLY NERVOUS, AND HIS OTHER MINISTERS INCREASINGLY JEALOUS.

PLAYING IT SAFE, TWO HOURS AFTER THE ASSASSINATION MUHAMMAD HAD SENT A DIRECTIVE TO ALL MOSQUE MINISTERS FORBIDDING THEM TO COMMENT ON THE ASSASSINATION.

NINE DAYS LATER, WITH THE POLITICAL CLIMATE STILL CHARGED AND EMOTIONS RAW, MUHAMMAD CANCELED A SPEAKING ENGAGEMENT IN NEW YORK CITY, SENDING MALCOLM IN HIS STEAD.

MALCOLM DELIVERED HIS SPEECH WITHOUT INCIDENT. BUT THE FIRST QUESTION FROM THE AUDIENCE WAS A REQUEST FOR HIS REACTION TO THE MURDER OF THE PRESIDENT. MALCOLM COULDN'T RESIST:

IT'S SIMPLY A CASE OF THE CHICKENS COMING HOME TO ROOST.

BEING AN OLD FARM BOY MYSELF, CHICKENS COMING HOME TO ROOST NEVER MADE ME SAD; THEY'VE ONLY MADE ME GLAD!

BACK IN CHICAGO, MUHAMMAD WAS RECORDING HIS OWN CONDOLENCE MESSAGE TO THE KENNEDY FAMILY WHEN HE WAS ASKED:

SO, MR. MUHAMMAD— WHAT'D YOU THINK ABOUT MALCOLM'S ASSASSINATION COMMENT THIS MORNING?

MUHAMMAD WAS INCREDULOUS. MALCOLM HAD DISOBEYED HIS DIRECTIVE. HE HAD TO BE PUNISHED.

THE NEXT MORNING, MALCOLM FLEW TO CHICAGO TO DISCUSS THE INCIDENT WITH MUHAMMAD.

THAT WAS A VERY BAD STATEMENT. THE COUNTRY LOVED THIS MAN. THE WHOLE NATION IS IN MOURNING.

THAT WAS VERY ILL-TIMED. A STATEMENT LIKE THAT CAN MAKE IT HARD ON MUSLIMS IN GENERAL.

I'LL HAVE TO SILENCE YOU FOR THE NEXT 90 DAYS—SO THAT MUSLIMS EVERYWHERE CAN BE DISASSOCIATED FROM YOUR BLUNDER.

SIR, I AGREE WITH YOU AND I SUBMIT, 100 PERCENT.

BY THE TIME MALCOLM RETURNED TO THE NEW YORK MOSQUE, HIS STUDENTS HAD ALREADY BEEN TOLD THE NEWS— AND MALCOLM DISCOVERED THAT MUHAMMAD NOW FORBADE HIM TO TEACH AS WELL.

W.125 ST. LENOX AVE.

NEW YORK NEWSPAPERS, RADIO, AND TELEVISION STATIONS WERE ALREADY REPORTING THE STORY.

IN THE TIME IT TOOK MALCOLM TO FLY HOME, HIS FALL FROM MUHAMMAD'S GRACE HAD BECOME PART OF THE PUBLIC RECORD.

THREE DAYS LATER, A BROTHER REPORTED TO MALCOLM A CONVERSATION HE HAD OVERHEARD.

IF YOU KNEW WHAT THE MINISTER DID, YOU'D GO OUT AND KILL HIM YOURSELF.

MALCOLM BEGAN TO FEAR THAT THE NOI MEANT TO KILL HIM AND ONLY ONE MAN COULD BE BEHIND IT.

HE DECIDED IT WAS TIME TO TAKE A VACATION.

DAYS LATER, MALCOLM RECEIVED A CALL FROM AN FOI MEMBER WHO SAID HE'D BEEN ASKED TO PUT A BOMB IN MALCOLM'S CAR. HE HAD REFUSED, AND HAD QUIT THE NOI.

MALCOLM CONSTANTLY TRAVELED ON BEHALF OF THE NOI, BUT THIS WAS HIS FIRST OPPORTUNITY TO VACATION WITH HIS YOUNG FAMILY. THEY HAD BEEN INVITED TO FLORIDA BY A TALENTED 22-YEAR-OLD BOXER NAMED CASSIUS CLAY.

CLAY WAS THERE TRAINING FOR HIS UPCOMING HEAVY-WEIGHT BOUT AGAINST THE CHAMPION, SONNY LISTON.

THANK YOU, BROTHER.

BUT MALCOLM AND HIS FAMILY WERE STILL IN DANGER.

WHEN HE WAS 17, CLAY'S BROTHER RUDY BROUGHT HIM TO THE NEW YORK MOSQUE TO HEAR MALCOLM PREACH.

AFTER CLAY HAD BECOME A REGULAR AT HIS TALKS, MALCOLM CONVINCED HIM TO JOIN THE NOI.

MALCOLM'S WIT, HUMOR, AND INTELLIGENCE CAPTIVATED CLAY; THE YOUNG FIGHTER WOULD BE SURE TO FIND A SEAT UP FRONT WHENEVER MALCOLM SPOKE.

FOR THREE YEARS NOW CLAY HAD BEEN A MEMBER OF THE NOI. HE KEPT IT A SECRET TO ALL BUT A FEW, AND CONTINUED USING HIS "SLAVE NAME."

A FIGHTER ON THE RISE HAD TO PLAY BY THE RULES, BUT AS A CHAMPION, HE'D WRITE HIS OWN.

AS CLAY ROSE IN THE BOXING WORLD, HIS RELATIONSHIP WITH MALCOLM BEGAN TO TROUBLE MUHAMMAD.

NOT ONLY WAS MUHAMMAD OPPOSED TO PROFESSIONAL BOXING BUT HE BELIEVED THAT CLAY WOULD LOSE HIS UPCOMING FIGHT AGAINST LISTON. HE DID NOT WANT THE NOI'S NAME ASSOCIATED WITH A FAILED FIGHTER.

MALCOLM, ON THE OTHER HAND, WAS CONVINCED THAT CLAY WAS DESTINED TO PULL OFF THE BOXING UPSET OF THE CENTURY.

IF HE WERE A BETTING MAN, MALCOLM WOULD HAVE BET THE FARM ON IT.

MALCOLM'S CONFIDENCE IN CLAY'S SKILLS ENERGIZED THE BOXER, AND HE ASKED MALCOLM TO BE HIS "SPIRITUAL ADVISER" IN THE DAYS LEADING UP TO THE FIGHT.

MALCOLM WAS READY TO HELP HIS FRIEND, EVEN IF IT MEANT VIOLATING HIS SILENCE ORDER.

FOR THE NIGHT OF THE FIGHT, MALCOLM REQUESTED SEAT NUMBER 7—HIS LUCKY NUMBER—HOPING IT WOULD ALSO INCREASE CLAY'S CHANCES OF VICTORY.

PERHAPS IT HELPED. ON FEBRUARY 25, 1964, CASSIUS CLAY DEFEATED SONNY LISTON TO BECOME THE YOUNGEST HEAVYWEIGHT CHAMPION IN HISTORY.

AFTER THE FIGHT, WITH THE RISK OF BEING ASSOCIATED WITH A "LOSER" GONE, MUHAMMAD CALLED CLAY AND GAVE HIM THE MUSLIM HOLY NAME MUHAMMAD INSTEAD OF THE USUAL X.

LATER, WHEN MALCOLM HEARD THE ANNOUNCEMENT THAT CASSIUS CLAY HAD BECOME MUHAMMAD ALI, HE LAUGHED. "THAT'S POLITICAL."

AT THE SAVIOURS' DAY SPEECH THE NEXT DAY, MUHAMMAD PROUDLY TOLD THE MEMBERS THAT HE HAD RENAMED CASSIUS CLAY AND THAT HIS FRIEND, THE CHAMP, WAS NOW A MEMBER OF THEIR ORGANIZATION.

ON MARCH 2, WHILE BEING INTERVIEWED ABOUT SOME OF THE "OUTRAGEOUS STATEMENTS" HE HAD MADE ABOUT ELIJAH MUHAMMAD'S DIVINE POWERS, ALI TOLD REPORTERS:

JUST WAIT TILL YOU HEAR WHAT MALCOLM IS GOING TO SAY IN A FEW DAYS.

ELIJAH MUHAMMAD WAS FURIOUS WHEN HE HEARD THIS. HE CALLED ALI, FORBIDDING HIM TO TALK TO MALCOLM, WHOSE SUSPENSION HE HAD MADE INDEFINITE.

ALI PROMISED TO END HIS FRIENDSHIP WITH MALCOLM. AS SAD AS IT MADE HIM, MALCOLM BORE ALI NO ILL WILL.

HE UNDERSTOOD THAT ALI WAS SIMPLY A PAWN IN MUHAMMAD'S GAME.

IT WAS CLEAR TO MALCOLM THAT HIS PLACE AT THE NOI TABLE WAS BEING CLEARED AWAY BY MEMBERS CONSPIRING AGAINST HIM.

AT THE SAVIOUR'S DAY CEREMONY, LOUIS X, BROUGHT INTO THE NOI BY MALCOLM HIMSELF, INTRODUCED THE MESSENGER TO THE AUDIENCE, AN HONORARY ACT MALCOLM USUALLY PERFORMED.

MALCOLM BELIEVED LOUIS AND OTHERS, ACTING OUT OF JEALOUSY, HAD CONVINCED MUHAMMAD THAT MALCOLM WAS CONSPIRING TO STEAL THE NOI LEADERSHIP FROM HIM.

DURING HIS SAVIOURS' DAY SERMON, MUHAMMAD SEEMED TO BE SINGLING MALCOLM OUT WHEN HE SAID:

ALLAH HAS MADE ME A DOOR. IF YOU GET OUT, YOU WILL COME BY ME, AND IF YOU REJECT ME, YOU WON'T GO. I HAVE BEEN GIVEN THE KEYS TO HEAVEN.

MALCOLM WROTE AND TELEPHONED MUHAMMAD THEN, DESPERATE TO SALVAGE THE RELATIONSHIP AND HIS STANDING IN THE NOI. MUHAMMAD'S REPLY WAS CURT.

YOU HAVE NOT OBEYED MY ORDER TO BE SILENT, SO NOW I WILL WAIT UNTIL YOU ARE QUIET BEFORE I GIVE YOU PERMISSION TO SPEAK IN PUBLIC.

IT WAS OVER NOW. FILLED WITH REGRET, MALCOLM HAD NO CHOICE BUT TO ACCEPT IT AND LOOK TO THE PROTECTION OF HIMSELF AND HIS FAMILY.

AND SO HE TOOK UP ARMS. AS HE HAD SAID IN HIS "MESSAGE TO THE GRASS ROOTS" JUST MONTHS BEFORE, "OUR RELIGION TEACHES US TO BE INTELLIGENT. BE PEACEFUL, BE COURTEOUS, OBEY THE LAW, RESPECT EVERYONE; BUT IF SOMEONE PUTS HIS HAND ON YOU, SEND HIM TO THE CEMETERY."

THERE WERE STILL SOME FRIENDS MALCOLM COULD COUNT ON, MEMBERS OF THE NOI WHO WOULD SIDE WITH HIM WHEN THE FINAL SPLIT BECAME PUBLIC.

CHARLES 37X, JAMES 67X, AND BENJAMIN GOODMAN AGREED THAT THEY WOULD FORM THE CORE OF THE NEW ORGANIZATION MALCOLM NOW PLANNED TO CREATE IN REACTION TO THE MESSENGER'S HYPOCRISY.

ON MARCH 8, MALCOLM CALLED A PRESS CONFERENCE TO ANNOUNCE THE FORMATION OF A NEW MUSLIM MOVEMENT, THE MUSLIM MOSQUE INCORPORATED.

THIS WILL GIVE US A RELIGIOUS BASE, AND THE SPIRITUAL FORCE NECESSARY TO RID OUR PEOPLE OF THE VICES THAT DESTROY THE MORAL FIBER OF OUR COMMUNITY.

WHILE MALCOLM MAINTAINED THE MMI WOULD WORK ALONGSIDE CIVIL RIGHTS GROUPS LIKE SNCC, CORE, AND NAACP, NONE REACHED OUT TO SUPPORT THIS NEW EFFORT.

BUT MALCOLM WASN'T WAITING. HE ANNOUNCED HE WOULD MAKE THE HAJJ—THE PILGRIMAGE TO THE SACRED CITY OF MECCA THAT ALL MUSLIMS MUST COMPLETE ONCE—AND TEACH THE KNOWLEDGE HE RECEIVED THERE TO HIS PEOPLE.

BUT THE TRIP WOULD COST MONEY— MONEY THAT, WITHOUT THE FINANCIAL SUPPORT OF THE NOI, MALCOLM DID NOT HAVE.

IN BOSTON, HE VISITED ELLA, THE ONE SIBLING HE COULD STILL COUNT ON. SHE HAD ONLY ONE QUESTION.

HOW MUCH DO YOU NEED?

DESPITE HIS SISTER'S HELP, MALCOLM MUST HAVE SUSPECTED THAT HIS FINANCIAL PROBLEMS WOULD DEEPEN WHEN HE RECEIVED A CERTIFIED LETTER FROM THE NOI TWO DAYS LATER.

THEY WANT THE HOUSE BACK...

THE LETTER STUNNED MALCOLM. THE HOUSE, HE WOULD INSIST, WAS A GIFT, PRACTICALLY FORCED ON HIM BY MUHAMMAD AFTER MALCOLM AND BETTY WED.

MALCOLM COULD NOT BELIEVE THAT MUHAMMAD WAS BEHIND THIS. THOSE CLOSEST TO HIM SAID MALCOLM LONGED FOR A RECONCILIATION.

IN HIS FRANTIC SPEAKING SCHEDULE, MALCOLM SENT CONFLICTING MESSAGES OF REPENTANCE AND DEFIANCE. HE TOLD EBONY MAGAZINE THAT THE BLACK MUSLIMS...

...CAN'T AFFORD TO LET ME LIVE...I KNOW WHERE THE BODIES ARE BURIED...

BUT DURING A PRESS CONFERENCE, HE RESISTED ENDORSING HIS OWN GROUP...

I WON'T TELL NEGROES TO COME AND FOLLOW ME. I'LL TELL THEM TO JOIN ANY ORGANIZATION WHERE BLACK NATIONALISM IS PRACTICED.

PERHAPS HE FELT THAT BY SIMPLY STAYING IN THE PUBLIC EYE, HE COULD KEEP THE NOI'S HENCHMEN AT BAY.

ON MARCH 26, MALCOLM WAS IN WASHINGTON, DC. THERE, THE CIVIL RIGHTS ACT CREATED UNDER PRESIDENT KENNEDY HAD FINALLY MADE IT INTO THE SENATE THANKS TO PRESIDENT LYNDON BAINES JOHNSON'S POLITICAL SAVVY.

INTRODUCED TO THE SENATE ON MARCH 6, IT WAS NOW THE SUBJECT OF A FILIBUSTER LAUNCHED BY SOUTHERN DEMOCRATS.

IF THE BILL WAS PASSED, MANY CIVIL RIGHTS ADVOCATES BELIEVED IT WOULD MARK A TURNING POINT FOR THEIR MOVEMENT.

MALCOLM DIDN'T NECESSARILY SHARE THAT OPINION, BUT HE SEEMED TO WANT TO PAY A VISIT TO SOMEONE WHO DID.

ONE OF THE MOST PROMINENT OF THE BILL'S SUPPORTERS HAPPENED TO BE IN THE CAPITOL BUILDING THAT DAY, SPEAKING TO THE PRESS IN THE HOPE OF BUILDING PUBLIC SUPPORT.

WHEN THE PRESS CONFERENCE CONCLUDED, MARTIN LUTHER KING DUCKED INTO THE HALL TO MAKE AN INCONSPICUOUS EXIT...

...BUT BUMPED RIGHT INTO MALCOLM INSTEAD.

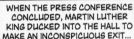

WELL, MALCOLM— GOOD TO SEE YOU!

GOOD TO SEE YOU!

IT'S NOT KNOWN IF MALCOLM ACTUALLY ORCHESTRATED THE QUIET YET HISTORIC MEETING, BUT A FEW PHOTOGRAPHERS WERE PRESENT TO RECORD IT— AND MALCOLM'S FINAL COMMENT:

NOW YOU'RE GOING TO GET INVESTIGATED!

IF MALCOLM HAD BEEN HOPING FOR A SIGN OF SUPPORT, HE DIDN'T GET IT. THE TWO WOULD NEVER MEET AGAIN.

THE FILIBUSTER WOULD GO ON TO BECOME ONE OF THE LONGEST IN SENATE HISTORY. PRESIDENT JOHNSON FINALLY SIGNED THE CIVIL RIGHTS ACT INTO LAW ON JULY 2, 1964.

AFTER RETURNING TO NEW YORK, MALCOLM LEARNED THAT MUHAMMAD HAD NOT ONLY REJECTED MALCOLM'S ATTEMPTS TO KEEP THE PEACE...

....HE HAD CALLED MALCOLM A "HYPOCRITE," WHICH, IN THE NOI CODE, WAS THE WORST CHARGE ONE COULD FORMALLY LEVEL AGAINST ANOTHER.

HE BROKE WITH ME, I DIDN'T BREAK WITH HIM! HE DON'T WANT ME!

THE NOI BROUGHT OUT PHILBERT X TO DENOUNCE HIS BROTHER, COMPARING HIM TO JUDAS AND BRUTUS. HE WENT EVEN FURTHER...

I AM AWARE OF THE MENTAL ILLNESS WHICH BESETTED MY MOTHER WHOM I LOVE, AND ONE OF MY OTHER BROTHERS, AND WHICH MAY NOW HAVE TAKEN ANOTHER VICTIM, MY BROTHER MALCOLM.

MALCOLM'S RESPONSE WAS TO REMAIN CALM AND FOCUSED. IN EARLY APRIL, HE GAVE THE FIRST VERSION OF A SPEECH HE WOULD USE OFTEN OVER THE COMING MONTHS.

FROM NOW ON, HE SAID, HE CONSIDERED RELIGION A PERSONAL MATTER. THEN HE GOT TO THE HEART OF HIS TALK: 1964 WOULD BE THE YEAR OF THE BALLOT... OR THE BULLET.

DESPITE ALL EFFORTS, VOTING INJUSTICE AND RACIAL BRUTALITY CONTINUED UNABATED. IN 1964, IF BLACKS DIDN'T GET THE BALLOT, IT WAS TIME FOR THE BULLET. BUT MALCOLM PROPOSED ANOTHER STRATEGY AS WELL.

SO OUR NEXT MOVE IS TO TAKE THE ENTIRE CIVIL RIGHTS STRUGGLE PROBLEM INTO THE UNITED NATIONS, AND LET THE WORLD SEE THAT UNCLE SAM IS GUILTY OF VIOLATING THE HUMAN RIGHTS OF 22 MILLION AFRO-AMERICANS.

CHAPTER ELEVEN: *HAJJ*

ON APRIL 13, 1964, MALCOLM X LEFT THE UNITED STATES, USING HIS FAMILY'S NEW NAME, EL-HAJJ MALIK EL-SHABAZZ.

MALCOLM ABANDONED HIS NOI SUIT, ADOPTING ROBES AND SANDALS. HE DID THE BEST HE COULD WITH NO ARABIC, RELYING ON THE KINDNESS OF FELLOW MUSLIMS.

NEVER HAVE I WITNESSED SUCH SINCERE HOSPITALITY AND OVERWHELMING SPIRIT OF TRUE BROTHERHOOD AS IS PRACTICED BY PEOPLE OF ALL COLORS AND RACES HERE IN THIS ANCIENT HOLY LAND, THE HOME OF ABRAHAM, MUHAMMAD, AND ALL THE OTHER PROPHETS OF THE HOLY SCRIPTURES.

I HAVE BEEN BLESSED TO VISIT THE HOLY CITY OF MECCA. I HAVE MADE MY SEVEN CIRCUITS AROUND THE KA'BA, LED BY A YOUNG MUTAWAF NAMED MUHAMMAD. I DRANK WATER FROM THE WELL OF THE ZAMZAM.

THERE WERE TENS OF THOUSANDS OF PILGRIMS FROM ALL OVER THE WORLD. THEY WERE OF ALL COLORS, FROM BLUE-EYED BLONDS TO BLACK-SKINNED AFRICANS.

BUT WE WERE ALL PARTICIPATING IN THE SAME RITUAL, DISPLAYING A SPIRIT OF UNITY AND BROTHERHOOD THAT MY EXPERIENCES IN AMERICA HAD LED ME TO BELIEVE NEVER COULD EXIST BETWEEN THE WHITE AND NONWHITE.

THROUGHOUT HIS STAY IN MECCA, HE WROTE ECSTATIC POSTCARDS TO THOSE AT HOME ABOUT THE RACIAL HARMONY HE WAS WITNESSING.

AMERICA NEEDS TO UNDERSTAND ISLAM, BECAUSE THIS IS THE ONE RELIGION THAT ERASES FROM ITS SOCIETY THE RACE PROBLEM. THROUGHOUT MY TRAVELS IN THE MUSLIM WORLD, I HAVE MET, TALKED TO, AND EVEN EATEN WITH PEOPLE WHO IN AMERICA WOULD HAVE BEEN CONSIDERED WHITE—

BUT THE WHITE ATTITUDE WAS REMOVED FROM THEIR MINDS BY THE RELIGION OF ISLAM. I HAVE NEVER BEFORE SEEN SINCERE AND TRUE BROTHER-HOOD PRACTICED BY ALL COLORS TOGETHER, IRRESPECTIVE OF THEIR COLOR.

YOU MAY BE SHOCKED BY THESE WORDS COMING FROM ME. BUT ON THIS PILGRIMAGE, WHAT I HAVE SEEN, AND EXPERIENCED, HAS FORCED ME TO REARRANGE MUCH OF MY THOUGHT PATTERNS PREVIOUSLY HELD, AND TO TOSS ASIDE SOME OF MY PREVIOUS CONCLUSIONS.

DURING THE PAST ELEVEN DAYS HERE IN THE MUSLIM WORLD, I HAVE EATEN FROM THE SAME PLATE, DRUNK FROM THE SAME GLASS, AND SLEPT ON THE SAME RUG—WHILE PRAYING TO THE SAME GOD—WITH FELLOW MUSLIMS, WHOSE EYES WERE THE BLUEST OF BLUE, WHOSE HAIR WAS THE BLONDEST OF BLOND, AND WHOSE SKIN WAS THE WHITEST OF WHITE.

WHEN ASKED WHAT HAD IMPRESSED HIM MOST ABOUT THE HAJJ, MALCOLM WOULD SAY, "THE BROTHERHOOD! THE PEOPLE OF ALL RACES, COLORS, FROM ALL OVER THE WORLD COMING TOGETHER AS ONE!"

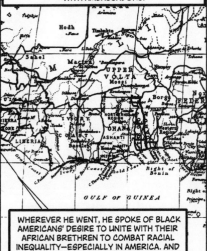

BUT AS MALCOLM'S OWN NOTES EMPHASIZE, HIS INABILITY TO SPEAK THE LANGUAGES OF THE MAJORITY OF HIS MUSLIM BROTHERS MEANT HE WAS ON THE OUTSIDE LOOKING IN. FROM THE INSIDE, HIS VISION OF UNIFIED HUMANITY WAS SOMETHING MUCH MORE COMPLICATED.

MALCOLM PROCEEDED TO VISIT LEBANON, EGYPT, GHANA, SENEGAL, NIGERIA, LIBERIA, MOROCCO, AND ALGERIA IN A WHIRLWIND OF SPEAKING ENGAGEMENTS AND AUDIENCES WITH AMBASSADORS.

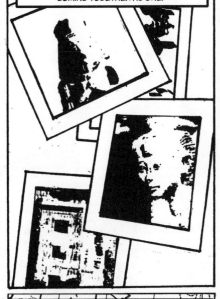

WHEREVER HE WENT, HE SPOKE OF BLACK AMERICANS' DESIRE TO UNITE WITH THEIR AFRICAN BRETHREN TO COMBAT RACIAL INEQUALITY—ESPECIALLY IN AMERICA. AND HE WAS MOVED BY THE RESPONSE.

THE AMERICAN NEGRO HAS NO CONCEPTION OF THE HUNDREDS OF MILLIONS OF OTHER NONWHITES' CONCERN FOR HIM: HE HAS NO CONCEPTION OF THEIR FEELINGS OF BROTHERHOOD FOR AND WITH HIM.

HE FOUND AFRICAN LEADERS MORE THAN READY TO JOIN WITH HIM TO BRING THE CASE OF THE UNITED STATES' BLACK CITIZENS BEFORE THE U.N.

NOT LONG AFTER RETURNING TO NEW YORK ON MAY 21, MALCOLM HELD A PRESS CONFERENCE TO DISCUSS THE TRIP WITH THE MEDIA.

ALTHOUGH AT FIRST REPORTERS SEEMED TO BE MORE INTERESTED IN HIS BEARD THAN HIS REVISED OPINIONS, HE QUICKLY FOCUSED ATTENTION ON HIS NEW RACIAL PHILOSOPHY.

DO WE CORRECTLY UNDERSTAND THAT YOU NOW DO NOT THINK THAT ALL WHITES ARE EVIL?

TRUE, SIR! MY TRIP TO MECCA HAS OPENED MY EYES. I NO LONGER SUBSCRIBE TO RACISM. I HAVE ADJUSTED MY THINKING TO THE POINT WHERE I BELIEVE WHITES ARE HUMAN BEINGS...

...AS LONG AS THIS IS BORNE OUT BY THEIR HUMANE ATTITUDE TOWARD NEGROES.

ON JUNE 28, AT THE HOTEL THERESA IN HARLEM, MALCOLM FORMALLY ANNOUNCED THE BIRTH OF THE ORGANIZATION OF AFRO-AMERICAN UNITY (OAAU), MODELED ON THE ORGANIZATION OF AFRICAN UNITY THAT HE'D BECOME ACQUAINTED WITH IN HIS TRAVELS.

THE GOAL OF THE OAAU WOULD BE TO IMPROVE THE CONDITIONS OF BLACK AMERICANS BY BUILDING THE INDEPENDENCE OF THE BLACK COMMUNITY, IN CONJUNCTION WITH AFRICANS AROUND THE WORLD.

MALCOLM WOULD SPEND MUCH OF THE TIME REMAINING TO HIM TRAVELING IN AFRICA AND EUROPE TO BOTH RALLY SUPPORT...

...AND STAY OUT OF THE SIGHTS OF HIS ENEMIES.

90

THAT JUNE, DASHING FROM BOSTON TO NEW YORK FOR HIS EVICTION HEARING ON JULY 13, MALCOLM LEFT BENJAMIN GOODMAN AND SIX AIDES TO TAKE CARE OF THE NEXT DAY'S APPOINTMENTS.

THE FOLLOWING DAY GOODMAN AND THE OTHERS WERE DRIVING TO THE AIRPORT WHEN THEY NOTICED TWO CARLOADS OF BLACK MEN FOLLOWING THEM.

THEY ATTEMPTED TO SPEED AWAY, BUT WERE CUT OFF INSIDE BOSTON'S CALLAHAN TUNNEL.

THREE MEN WIELDING KNIVES EMERGED FROM THEIR CAR AND CAME AT GOODMAN.

WE'RE GOING TO KILL HIM! YOU'RE NOT GOING TO GET OUT OF HERE ALIVE!

BUT WHEN ONE OF MALCOLM'S AIDES POINTED A SHOTGUN OUT THE WINDOW AT THE KNIFE-WIELDING THUGS, THEY RAN OFF.

AFTERWARD MALCOLM NOTED, "THERE IS NO GROUP IN THE UNITED STATES MORE ABLE TO CARRY OUT THIS THREAT THAN THE BLACK MUSLIMS. I KNOW, BECAUSE I TAUGHT THEM MYSELF."

91

BUT AT THE TIME, MALCOLM WAS STRUGGLING IN A NYC COURTROOM TO PREVENT THE NOI FROM SEIZING HIS FAMILY'S HOME.

MALCOLM'S CASE RESTED ON TWO NOTIONS. FIRST, THAT THE HOUSE HAD BEEN GIVEN TO HIM, EVEN THOUGH THE DEED REMAINED IN THE NOI'S NAME; AND SECOND, THAT SINCE MALCOLM HAD NEVER BEEN FORMALLY FIRED, THE HOUSE REMAINED HIS TO KEEP.

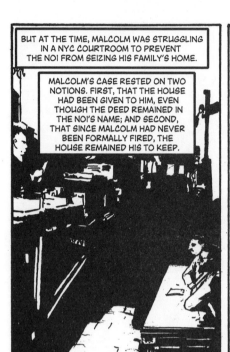

WHEN IT APPEARED THAT THE JUDGE WASN'T BUYING MALCOLM'S ARGUMENT, HE DECIDED TO USE THE TRIAL FOR ANOTHER PURPOSE—BRINGING MUHAMMAD'S SEXUAL TRESPASSES BEFORE THE PUBLIC.

MALCOLM KNEW THAT ANYTHING SAID IN COURT IN RELATION TO HIS DEFENSE WAS PRIVILEGED AGAINST LITIGATION FOR LIBEL OR SLANDER. HIS STATEMENT WOULD BE ENTERED INTO THE PUBLIC RECORD.

THIS WAS THE REASON I WAS SUSPENDED: MY MOUTH WAS CLOSED SO THAT I COULDN'T TALK!

YOUR HONOR! I OBJECT!

AS EXPECTED, THE JUDGE RULED THAT THE HOME WAS INDEED OWNED BY THE NOI, AND THAT MALCOLM AND HIS FAMILY HAD TO LEAVE.

THE LOSS WAS OFFSET BY A PERSONAL VICTORY. MALCOLM'S TESTIMONY MEANT THAT NEWSPAPERS COVERING THE STORY COULD TELL OF MUHAMMAD'S INDISCRETIONS NOW.

WHEN HE ARRIVED HOME THAT EVENING, MALCOLM DISCOVERED THAT HIS PHONE HAD GONE DEAD.

AT THE MMI OFFICE, THE STAFF PANICKED WHEN THEIR CALLS TO MALCOLM'S HOUSE WERE MET WITH A DISCONNECT RECORDING.

A GROUP OF THEM HOPPED IN A CAR AND RACED OVER TO THE X HOME—TO FIND MALCOLM AND HIS FAMILY UNDISTURBED.

THE PHONE COMPANY SAID A "MRS. SMALL" HAD CALLED, AND CLAIMING THAT SHE WAS LEAVING ON VACATION, HAD ASKED FOR HER PHONE TO BE DISCONNECTED.

RELIEVED, THE GROUP RETURNED TO HARLEM, STOPPING TO PICK UP A NEWSPAPER. THEY HAD FORGOTTEN, HOWEVER THAT THE NEWSSTAND WAS JUST NEXT-DOOR TO THE NOI'S RESTAURANT.

AN NOI MEMBER SAW THE GROUP AND THREW A PUNCH; OTHERS RAN TO SUPPORT HIM. ONE OF MALCOLM'S GROUP PULLED A GUN FROM THE CAR.

A FIGHT BROKE OUT, WHICH WAS STOPPED ONLY BY THE ARRIVAL OF THE POLICE. WEAPONS WERE SEIZED AND SIX OF MALCOLM'S MEN WERE ARRESTED.

AFTER THIS SERIES OF SUSPICIOUS INCIDENTS, MALCOLM THOUGHT IT SAFER TO LEAVE THE COUNTRY AND DEVOTE HIMSELF TO BUILDING SUPPORT FOR THE OAAU.

SHORTLY AFTER HIS RETURN, IN JANUARY OF 1965, HE FLEW TO LOS ANGELES TO SPEAK WITH TWO OF MUHAMMAD'S SECRETARIES WHO HAD FILED PATERNITY SUITS.

FRIENDS PICKED MALCOLM UP AT THE AIRPORT AND DROVE HIM TO THE HOTEL.

AS THEY ENTERED THE LOBBY, SIX MEN FOLLOWED THEM IN, THEN WATCHED MALCOLM GO UP TO HIS ROOM AND WAITED IN THE LOBBY. ONE FRIEND RECOGNIZED THEM AS NOI MEMBERS.

WHEN MALCOLM RETURNED TO THE LOBBY HE PRACTICALLY BUMPED INTO THE NOI ENTOURAGE.

MALCOLM'S FACE FROZE, BUT HE NEVER BROKE HIS GAIT AS HE LEFT THE HOTEL.

AFTER MEETING THE SECRETARIES AND GETTING THEIR SWORN DEPOSITIONS, MALCOLM AND HIS FRIENDS ATE DINNER AND WENT BACK TO THE HOTEL.

WHEN THEY ARRIVED, ONE FRIEND SAID, "BLACK MUSLIMS WERE ALL OVER THE PLACE. THEY HAD THE HOTEL COMPLETELY SURROUNDED."

MALCOLM RACED PAST THEM, AND DID NOT LEAVE HIS ROOM UNTIL IT WAS TIME TO FLY TO HIS NEXT DESTINATION: CHICAGO.

THE FOLLOWING MORNING, AS HE DROVE MALCOLM TO THE AIRPORT, HIS FRIEND NOTICED THEY WERE BEING FOLLOWED.

"HARDLY HAD WE GOT ON THE FREEWAY WHEN WE SAW TWO CARLOADS OF NOI GUYS FOLLOWING US," THE FRIEND REMEMBERED.

AS THE CARS BEGAN TO PULL UP ALONGSIDE MALCOLM, HE REACHED DOWN TO PICK UP A WALKING STICK KEPT ON THE FLOOR.

WHEN HE SLIPPED IT OUT THE WINDOW, HOLDING IT AS IF IT WERE A SHOTGUN, AND POINTED IT AT ONE NOI CAR, THE DRIVER SWERVED OFF IN TERROR.

MALCOLM'S FRIEND'S FOOT DIDN'T STEP OFF THE GAS UNTIL THEY'D ARRIVED AT THE DEPARTURE GATE.

ARRIVALS DEPARTURES

MALCOLM HAD COME TO CHICAGO TO TESTIFY IN THE STATE OF ILLINOIS' INVESTIGATIONS OF THE NOI.

AFTER HIS PLANE TOUCHED DOWN AT O'HARE AIRPORT, POLICE ESCORTED MALCOLM TO HIS HOTEL. OFFICERS STATIONED IN THE NEXT ROOM KEPT HIM UNDER 24-HOUR GUARD.

MALCOLM ACCEPTED THEIR PROTECTION. AFTER ALL, CHICAGO WAS THE HOME BASE OF THE NOI. THE CHICAGO POLICE KNEW WHAT THE NOI WAS CAPABLE OF.

AFTER HIS FINAL DAY OF TESTIMONY, MALCOLM RETURNED TO HIS HOTEL TO FIND 15 GRIM-FACED BLACK MEN LOITERING NEARBY, AT LEAST TWO OF WHOM MALCOLM RECOGNIZED AS NOI MEMBERS.

BACK IN HIS ROOM, MALCOLM SPOKE TO A DETECTIVE.

IT'S ONLY A MATTER OF TIME BEFORE THEY CATCH UP WITH ME. I KNOW TOO MUCH ABOUT THE MUSLIMS. BUT THEIR THREATS ARE NOT GOING TO STOP ME FROM WHAT I AM DETERMINED TO DO.

THE NEXT MORNING, THE POLICE ESCORTED MALCOLM TO THE PLANE THAT WOULD TAKE HIM BACK TO NEW YORK.

HE WAS HOME JUST LONG ENOUGH TO RECEIVE THE NOTICE OF EVICTION FROM HIS HOUSE.

NOTICE OF EVICTION

THEN HE WAS OFF ON ANOTHER WEEK OF SPEECHES. PAYMENTS FOR SPEAKING ENGAGEMENTS, ALONG WITH ADVANCES ON HIS AUTOBIOGRAPHY, WERE NOW THE ONLY SOURCE OF INCOME FOR MALCOLM AND HIS FAMILY.

BAROOMM!

ON FEBRUARY 14, MALCOLM HAD THE RARE OPPORTUNITY TO SLEEP IN HIS OWN BED... BUT AT 3 A.M. HE WAS AWAKENED BY AN EXPLOSION.

MALCOLM AND BETTY SNATCHED UP THEIR FOUR CHILDREN AND FLED THE HOUSE.

WHEN THE FIRE DEPARTMENT ARRIVED IT TOOK THEM AN HOUR TO EXTINGUISH THE BLAZE, WHICH THEY SAID WAS CAUSED BY A MOLOTOV COCKTAIL BEING HURLED THROUGH THE FRONT PICTURE WINDOW.

MALCOLM WAS CERTAIN THAT THE NATION OF ISLAM WAS RESPONSIBLE. BUT THE SIGHT OF THE BLAZING HOUSE MAY ALSO HAVE REMINDED HIM OF THAT LONG-AGO NIGHT IN LANSING, MICHIGAN, WHEN THE BLACK LEGION BURNED DOWN THE FIRST PLACE HE COULD REMEMBER AS HOME.

DAYS LATER, WITH HIS WIFE AND CHILDREN SAFE AT A FRIEND'S HOME, MALCOLM RENTED A ROOM AT THE NEW YORK HILTON HOTEL.

THE BELLMAN ACCOMPANIED HIM TO A ROOM ON THE 12TH FLOOR.

A SHORT TIME LATER, SOME BLACK MEN ENTERED THE HOTEL LOBBY, ASKING ALL THE BELLMEN WHAT ROOM MALCOLM X WAS STAYING IN.

LIKE MOST NEW YORKERS, THE HOTEL STAFF KNEW THAT MALCOLM HAD BEEN TARGETED FOR ASSASSINATION, SO THE BELLMEN WERE IMMEDIATELY SUSPICIOUS.

THEY CONTACTED SECURITY, WHICH IMMEDIATELY ADDED STAFF TO GUARD MALCOLM ON THE 12TH FLOOR.

THAT EVENING, MALCOLM LEFT HIS ROOM ONLY TO EAT DINNER IN THE HOTEL RESTAURANT BEFORE GOING TO BED FOR THE NIGHT.

ON SUNDAY, FEBRUARY 21, BETTY SHABAZZ, NOW PREGNANT WITH TWINS, WAS AWAKENED AT 9 A.M. BY A CALL FROM HER HUSBAND. HE WANTED TO KNOW IF IT WOULD BE TOO MUCH TROUBLE FOR HER TO BRING THE CHILDREN TO THE 2 P.M. MEETING AT THE AUDUBON BALLROOM IN HARLEM.

OF COURSE IT WON'T!

ALTHOUGH MALCOLM HAD SAID THAT THE MEETING WOULD BE TOO DANGEROUS FOR BETTY AND THE GIRLS TO ATTEND, SOMETHING MADE HIM WANT TO SEE THEM AGAIN DESPITE THE RISK.

YOU KNOW WHAT HAPPENED AN HOUR AGO? EXACTLY AT EIGHT O'CLOCK, THE PHONE WOKE ME UP. SOME MAN SAID "WAKE UP, BROTHER," AND HUNG UP.

ALTHOUGH MALCOLM FEARED THE WORST, HE MADE NO SECURITY ARRANGEMENTS. AS ALWAYS AT MMI AND OAAU MEETINGS, NO ONE WAS FRISKED — THAT WAS TOO MUCH IN THE STYLE OF THE NOI FOR MALCOLM.

ONE WOMAN NOTED THAT A FEW SEATS NEAR THE FRONT HAD BEEN CLAIMED EARLY, BUT THAT WASN'T UNUSUAL WHEN THE MINISTER WAS SPEAKING.

GUEST SPEAKERS HADN'T SHOWN UP, AND MALCOLM SEEMED DEEPLY DISAPPOINTED. A FILL-IN SPEAKER WENT OUT TO PLAY FOR TIME. NOW IT WAS 3:08. MALCOLM COULDN'T KEEP THE AUDIENCE WAITING ANY LONGER.

AS SALAAM ALAIKUM, BROTHERS AND SISTERS!

A FEW ROWS FROM THE FRONT, A COMMOTION STARTED, AND AS ATTENTION TURNED AWAY FROM THE STAGE...

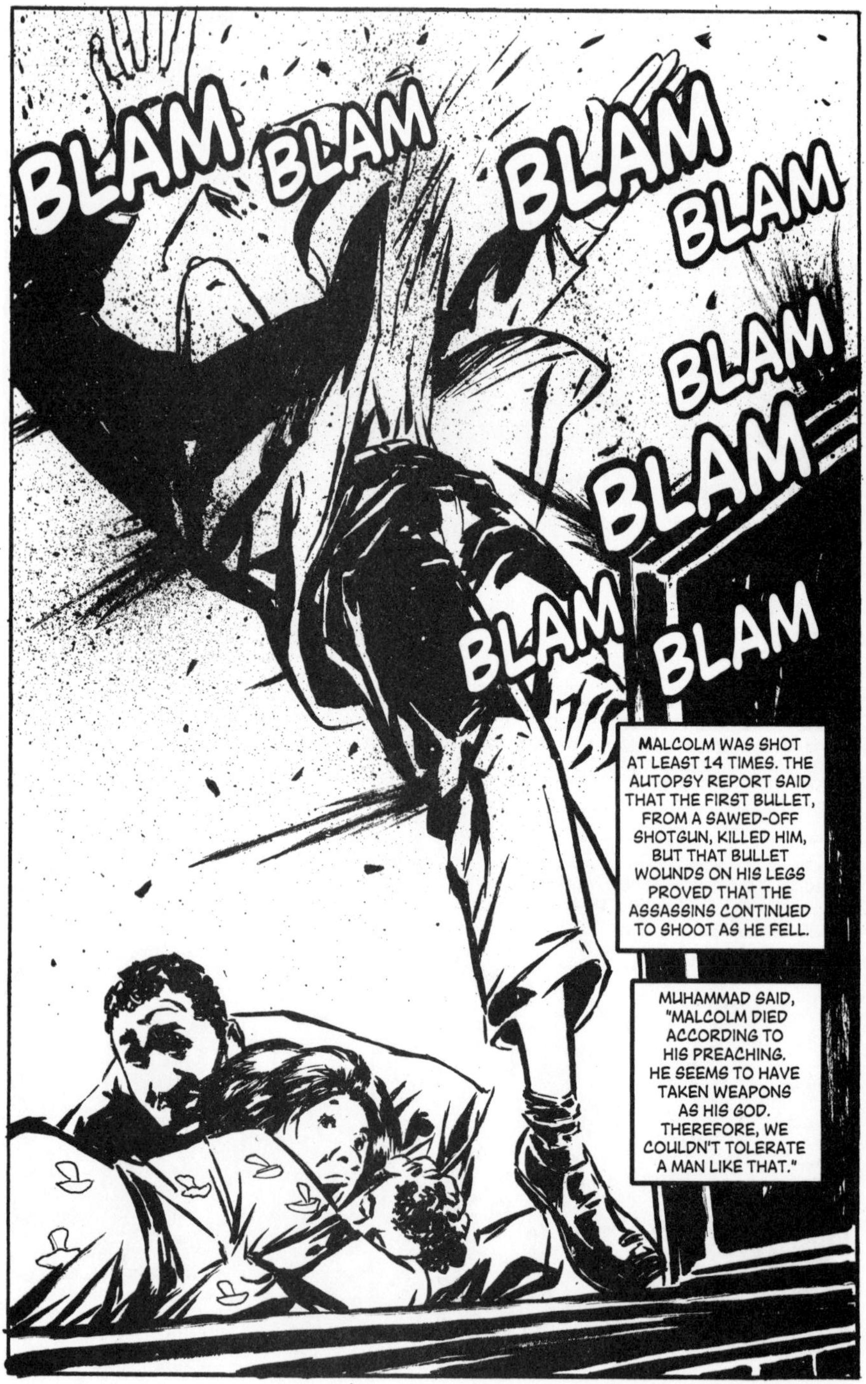
BLAM
BLAM
BLAM
BLAM
BLAM
BLAM
BLAM
BLAM
MALCOLM WAS SHOT AT LEAST 14 TIMES. THE AUTOPSY REPORT SAID THAT THE FIRST BULLET, FROM A SAWED-OFF SHOTGUN, KILLED HIM, BUT THAT BULLET WOUNDS ON HIS LEGS PROVED THAT THE ASSASSINS CONTINUED TO SHOOT AS HE FELL.
MUHAMMAD SAID, "MALCOLM DIED ACCORDING TO HIS PREACHING. HE SEEMS TO HAVE TAKEN WEAPONS AS HIS GOD. THEREFORE, WE COULDN'T TOLERATE A MAN LIKE THAT."

MORE THAN 20,000 PEOPLE STOOD IN LINE OUTSIDE HARLEM'S UNITY FUNERAL HOME TO PAY THEIR LAST RESPECTS TO MALCOLM, WHO HAD BEEN PREPARED FOR BURIAL WITH THE TRADITIONAL MUSLIM OILS AND ROBES.

TALMADGE HAYER, NORMAN 2X BUTLER, AND THOMAS 15X JOHNSON WERE ARRESTED FOR THE MURDER. ALL WERE MEMBERS OF THE NOI.

THE FOLLOWING YEAR, ALL THREE MEN WERE TRIED AND CONVICTED OF THE ASSASSINATION. BUT TO THIS DAY, QUESTIONS REMAIN; NOT OVER WHO COMMITTED THE CRIME, BUT OVER WHAT THEIR MOTIVES WERE.

WAS MALCOLM'S MURDER, AS SOME SAY, PART OF AN FBI PLOT? OR WAS IT, AS OTHERS BELIEVE, COMMISSIONED BY CERTAIN HIGH-RANKING MEMBERS OF THE NOI? OR WAS IT SIMPLY, YET HORRIBLY, A VIOLENT ACT OF REVENGE FOR A PERCEIVED BETRAYAL BY A ONCE-REVERED LEADER?

IN THE END, THE ONLY CERTAINTY MAY BE THAT AMERICA HAD LOST ONE OF ITS MOST ORIGINAL AND OUTSPOKEN LEADERS.

IN A CONVERSATION WITH AUTHOR ALEX HALEY DURING THE WRITING OF HIS AUTOBIOGRAPHY, MALCOLM SPECULATED ON HIS PROSPECTS FOR INFLUENCING THE LIVES OF AFRICAN AMERICANS:

"BROTHER, DO YOU REALIZE THAT SOME OF HISTORY'S GREATEST LEADERS NEVER WERE RECOGNIZED UNTIL THEY WERE SAFELY IN THE GROUND!"

BUT, IN DELIVERING THE EULOGY AT MALCOLM'S FUNERAL, ACTOR OSSIE DAVIS OFFERED PERHAPS THE MOST MOVING TESTAMENT TO MALCOLM'S LEGACY:

"MALCOLM WAS OUR MANHOOD, OUR LIVING, BLACK MANHOOD! THIS WAS HIS MEANING TO HIS PEOPLE. AND, IN HONORING HIM, WE HONOR THE BEST IN OURSELVES... CONSIGNING THESE MORTAL REMAINS TO EARTH, THE COMMON MOTHER OF ALL, SECURE IN THE KNOWLEDGE THAT WHAT WE PLACE IN THE GROUND IS NO MORE NOW A MAN – BUT A SEED – WHICH, AFTER THE WINTER OF OUR DISCONTENT, WILL COME FORTH AGAIN TO MEET US. AND WE WILL KNOW HIM THEN FOR WHAT HE WAS AND IS – A PRINCE – OUR OWN BLACK SHINING PRINCE! – WHO DIDN'T HESITATE TO DIE, BECAUSE HE LOVED US SO."

SELECT PHOTOGRAPHIC REFERENCES

ABOVE LEFT Typical southern sharecroppers' home, 1922 (General Research and Reference Division, Schomburg Center, The New York Public Library)

ABOVE RIGHT The great northern migration of African Americans (Photographs and Prints Division, Schomburg Center, The New York Public Library)

ABOVE Harlem street, mid-1940s (Photographs and Prints Division, Schomburg Center, The New York Public Library)

LEFT Police mug shot of Malcolm X, 1944 (© Bettmann/Corbis)

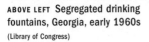

ABOVE LEFT Segregated drinking fountains, Georgia, early 1960s (Library of Congress)

ABOVE RIGHT Sit-down strike at a segregated luncheon counter, 1960 (Library of Congress)

RIGHT Martin Luther King Jr. and Malcolm X, March 1964 (Library of Congress)

BELOW Malcolm X on stretcher following assassination, 1965 (Library of Congress)

FURTHER READING

Breitman, George, ed. *Malcolm X Speaks: Selected Speeches and Statements.* New York: Grove Press, 1990.

Brown, Kevin. *Malcolm X: His Life and Legacy.* Brookfield, Conn.: Milbrook Press, 1995.

DeCaro, Louis A., Jr. *On the Side of My People: A Religious Life of Malcolm X.* New York: New York University Press, 1997.

Friedly, Michael. *Malcolm X: The Assassination.* New York: Ballantine Books, 1995.

Gallen, David. *Malcolm X: As They Knew Him.* New York: Ballantine Books, 1995.

Gallen, David, Benjamin Karim, and Peter Skutches. *Remembering Malcolm.* New York: One World/Ballantine Books, 1995.

Haley, Alex and Malcolm X. *The Autobiography of Malcolm X.* New York: Penguin Books, 2004.

Jenkins, Robert L. and Mfanya Donald Tryman, eds. *The Malcolm X Encyclopedia.* Westport, Conn.: Greenwood Press, 2002.

Perry, Bruce. *Malcolm: The Life of the Man Who Changed Black America.* Barrytown, N. Y.: Station Hill Press, 1991.